AF322631

THE TRINITY TRILOGY

AN INVITATION TO GAZE UPON THE EXQUISITE BEAUTY OF THE TRIUNE GOD

THE
TRINITY
TRILOGY

AN INVITATION TO GAZE UPON THE EXQUISITE BEAUTY OF THE TRIUNE GOD

MARK MEDLEY

The Trinity Trilogy
An Invitation to Gaze Upon the Exquisite Beauty of a Triune God

© 2024 Mark Medley

Printed in the United States of America.

Published in Knoxville, Tennessee, through IngramSpark.

Cover & Interior Design by Morgan Schutz
Edited by Grace Schutz

ISBN: (Hardcover) 979-8-3305-2239-2
ISBN: (ebook) 979-8-3305-2240-8

To Katie, Ally, Emily, and Zac

The Trinity Trilogy is three books in one volume that explores the depths of each member of the Triune God. Each book contains 30 days of devotional readings that shine light on the person, heart, and work of the Father, the Son, and the Holy Spirit.

Book One, *The Glory of the Father in the Face of Jesus Christ*, is a study of who the Father is and what he is like from the perspective of the life of Jesus Christ. It is a journey from an orphan-hearted existence to living as beloved sons and daughters of our Heavenly Father.

Book Two, *Irresistible Jesus*, is a study of the gospels that helps us better understand the person and works of Jesus Christ from the vantage point of his disciples. What is it about this Man that would cause them to leave everything and give their lives for him?

Book Three, *The Promise of the Father*, explores the power and purpose of the Holy Spirit as discovered in his activity in the lives of believers in the early church.

My desire is that these devotions will:

- Help us better understand, love, and long for intimacy with the Triune God.

- Challenge the narratives we have all developed for each member of the Trinity.

- Spark wonder in our hearts, leading to a life-giving, day-to-day relationship with God.

THE GLORY OF THE FATHER

IN THE FACE OF JESUS CHRIST

BOOK ONE

INTRODUCTION

BOOK ONE

What is God like? What does he think about me?

These are some of the most important questions you will ever ask. And God has not left us without answers.

Jesus Christ said, "Whoever has seen me has seen the Father." (John 14:9b) He is the express image of the living God (Hebrews 1:1–4). In his life on Earth, Jesus opened to us the thoughts, words, passions, and actions of God the Father and displayed how they can affect our souls and touch our lives in real ways every day.

This book is a 30-day journey through the gospels to encounter the glory of the Father in the face of Jesus Christ. But it also reveals the path we all can take from an orphan-hearted existence to living as beloved sons and daughters of God.

Orphans live from a perspective of fear, scarcity, and inadequacy, experiencing thoughts such as "I don't have enough," and "I am not enough." Sons and daughters are truly and vitally connected to their Father and experience extraordinary love and peace. This changes their perspective and impacts the world around them.

Jesus revealed the Father, not only as a sovereign Lord, outside and beyond us, but also as a loving Father, relational and near to us. Holding these two truths in balance steadies us, establishes us, and sets us up with all we need in order to know the Father and to make him known to others.

DAILY READINGS

Day 1 — God of Generations — *Matthew 1:1–17*
Day 2 — God of Providence — *Matthew 2:1–23*
Day 3 — Orphans & Sons — *Matthew 3:1–17*
Day 4 — Resting & Risking — *Matthew 4:1–3*
Day 5 — The Highest Calling — *Matthew 4:3–11*
Day 6 — An Upside-Down Kingdom — *Matthew 5:1–48*
Day 7 — More Valuable Than My Sin — *Mark 1:11–15*
Day 8 — God of the Dance — *John 5:16–30*
Day 9 — Living Loved — *Matthew 7:1–29*
Day 10 — God Who Gives It Away — *Matthew 10:1–42*
Day 11 — God of Rest — *Mark 6:30–32*
Day 12 — God Who Speaks & Listens — *Luke 11:1–13*
Day 13 — God to Be Worshiped — *John 4:1–26*
Day 14 — Proud Father — *Mark 9:2–8*
Day 15 — God Who Disciplines — *Matthew 11:1–30*
Day 16 — God Most High — *Matthew 12:1–50*
Day 17 — Moved by Compassion — *Matthew 14:1–36*
Day 18 — God the Just — *Matthew 20:1–34*
Day 19 — God of Kindness & Severity —
    Mark 2:1—3:35
Day 20 — How Orphans Live — *Matthew 23:1–39*
Day 21 — God of Open Arms — *Matthew 11:25–30*
Day 22 — God of the Heart — *Mark 7:1–30*
Day 23 — God of Legacy — *Matthew 19:23–30*
Day 24 — God of Purpose — *John 15:1–27*
Day 25 — God of My Darkest Days — *John 17:1–26*

GOD OF GENERATIONS

DAY 1 | *MATTHEW 1:1–17*

The New Testament begins with a family tree. God cares for each generation, but he also cares for the long game. His plan is bigger than we realize, and looking back gives us our bearings for what God is doing now and where he is taking us.

Jesus was born into a context—not just the historical context of first-century Palestine, but the context of his Father's covenant with Israel. In the fullness of time, the Son came to fulfill the Father's promise. Jesus was a vital part of his Father's plan even before his birth on Earth: He was the seed of Abraham, the end of David's regal line, and the second Adam who redeems the first Adam's fall.

God is the perfect Father, but he is more than that. He is a God of generations. Throughout the Old Testament, he reveals himself as the God of Abraham, Issac, and Jacob. He keeps covenant and shows mercy to a thousand generations. Generations are not just how he works; they are who he is, for there are even generations (Father and Son) within the Trinity itself!

In this genealogy in Matthew 1, we find liars, adulterers, idol-worshipers, and prostitutes. God chooses to work his plan through generations of sinful men and women. He weaves the abused and the abusers alike into a tapestry of his redemptive purpose. He works through you and me as well. Our perfect Father uses weak and sinful fathers and mothers to bring sons and daughters into his kingdom on Earth.

Never make the mistake of despising yourself or your family tree. Your Father is bigger than your lineage.

- How aware am I that God has brought me into his family and become a Father to me? How does this truth affect my daily life?

- What limitations have I placed on myself because of my own family? How might God be challenging my mindset about this? How has God already worked his redemption in my family of origin?

DIG DEEPER · *Romans 8:14–17; Genesis 17:3–8*

God of Generations, you have worked through Jesus to bring many sons and daughters to yourself. You have put your Spirit in my heart crying, "Abba, Father!" As Jesus was one with you and one with your purpose, help me to see that you are drawing me into your heart and mission.

GOD OF PROVIDENCE

DAY 2 | *MATTHEW 2:1–23*

The Father worked his purposes while the infant Jesus was nursing, while the toddler Jesus was sleeping. Big wheels are turning all around us in the heavenly spheres, mostly unperceived by us, as our Father guides and cares for us.

We understand Jesus' birth as miraculous; the God of eternity coming to us, finite and fleshly—the unveiling of the Son who had always existed with the Father. But we often fail to see that once he was here, Jesus was miraculously covered by his Father, who worked in many ways through many agents.

He used the wisdom of Jesus' earthly father and mother, the insight of wise men, the testimony of scriptures, signs in the heavens, and dreams in the night. He literally moved Heaven and Earth in order to preserve his Son and his Son's destiny. And all of this happened without the babe's awareness.

Jesus' life introduces us to an amazing life of rest in the strong hands of our Father. We can trust our future to him. We can trust our children to him. We can be confident that he is at work even when we aren't aware of it.

If we are listening, our Father gives us a fresh adjustment in our perspective each evening. We are reminded that we cannot sleep unless we relinquish control and concede that our world will be alright without our input for a few hours.

In the same way, we can live our waking moments in rest, knowing that the God of dreams, kings, and stars holds us.

- In what areas of my life do I tend to grasp for control? Are these areas sources of anxiety in my life?
- In what ways have I seen God's sovereign hand at work protecting what concerns me?

DIG DEEPER · *PSALM 138:6–8; MATTHEW 6:25–34*

*God of Providence, nothing escapes your watchful eye.
As the universe rests in your control—as the Holy Child
slept while all around him wrestled and nestled into your
plan—let me rest in your care for me.*

ORPHANS & SONS

DAY 3 | *MATTHEW 3:1–17*

This chapter sets the stage for the great struggle of the gospel throughout Jesus' ministry—even throughout the ages. Two great adversaries contend in this epic battle: the orphan-hearted and the true sons and daughters.

Those who trusted their own righteousness said, "We have Abraham as our father." This was their way of saying, "We are right with God because of our ancestors and our hard work of keeping the law." But the law was powerless to bring them—or us—into a relationship with God.

The contrast couldn't be greater: An orphan heart fights for itself, trusts in itself, carries its own burden. Sons and daughters are in relationship through the Father's initiating love and pleasure.

And now, after thousands of years of promises and hundreds of years of silence, the Father declares the inauguration of the King of his great kingdom. But when he announces this King, he doesn't say, "This is my long-awaited Messiah." He doesn't declare sternly, "This is the Creator and Judge of Heaven and Earth; bow before him."

No, the voice from Heaven said, "This is my Son…I love him…I am pleased with him."

Jesus lived and ministered out of this place of sonship, acceptance, and security. From the very beginning—before he did any miracles, before his teachings, before his obedience unto death on the cross—Jesus was able to obey, to endure, to give all because of his identity and intimacy with the Father. From day one, the entire enterprise was fueled by relationship.

"Yes, but that was Jesus," you may say, "of course he is the Son of God." You are right, and yet the wonder is that we too are in Christ, "accepted in the Beloved" (Ephesians 1:5–6, NKJV). Our union with Christ means that we share the very acceptance and intimacy that Jesus enjoyed with his Father.

We are no longer orphan-hearted. We are children of God through Christ, and this changes everything.

- If I were confident that my righteousness was not dependent on me, how would that change my life today?

- How does knowing God as Father change how I think about what I am facing today?

DIG DEEPER · *GALATIANS 4:4–7; 1 JOHN 3:1–3; EPHESIANS 1:1–14*

Father, help me to comprehend that through your Beloved Son you have made me your child also. Deliver me from the mindset of an orphan. Teach me what it means to be a child of my Father.

RESTING & RISKING

DAY 4   *MATTHEW 4:1–3*

If I can rest, I can risk.

Jesus, knowing he was not an orphan but a beloved Son, followed the Spirit's leading into the wilderness. He followed into a lonely, dangerous place where no food or water was promised because he knew his Father's heart. His relationship with the Father infused him with trust.

Sons can take risks when they feel a nudge of the Spirit. Orphans count the cost and shrink back. Daughters walk in step with him, trusting the provision will come. Orphans wrestle with scarcity. Which way of thinking is natural to you?

The first words of the accuser are telling: "If you are the Son of God..." This was no mere temptation to sin. It was an attack on Jesus' identity. He uses the same tactics on us. If the enemy can make us question our identity, the door to sin is wide open.

My Father's voice speaks life to me, calms me, and grounds me in my true identity. It is a bedrock on which I can build a new life. It is an anchor no matter how fierce the storm. My Father is not distraught, and I need not be either.

Resting and risking are proportional; I will risk exactly as much as I am resting in the love of my Father. Often we do not ask God to extend his hand because we do not know his heart. If I am convinced of the greatness of his heart for me, I can step out in faith to the task set before me. I can be bold in my witness for Christ. I can face uncertainty with courage.

Every day, Jesus lived out the very life of abiding that he called his followers to (John 15:3–4). Living in this union with Christ makes us brave, resolute, and courageous. It doesn't depend on our faith, but on his faithfulness.

- What new and unknown lands is my Father calling me to? What are the comfortable shores I must leave behind? Do I believe my Father is trustworthy?

- How does knowing that a good-hearted Father is loving and leading me change my decisions today?

DIG DEEPER · *Joshua 1:6–9; Proverbs 28:1*

Father, ground me in the deep and fertile soil of your love so I might hear your voice and venture into lands of obedience.

THE HIGHEST CALLING

DAY 5 | *MATTHEW 4:3–11*

Spiritual warfare is real. But our battle is more about our identity than our ability to fight.

When the devil arrived to tempt Jesus, the first words from his mouth revealed his strategy: *"If you are the Son of God..."* His assault was leveled on Jesus' identity as a Son of his Father. Jesus battled the enemy on three fronts:

- "Rely on your own ability." In effect, the tempter was saying, "You could not be the Son of God. God's Son would not be left hungry. He has abandoned you. Besides, God helps those who help themselves, so use your power to meet your own needs." But all of this is orphan thinking. True children know who they are because they know whose they are.

- "Show people how special you are." When Satan's self-reliance tactic didn't work, he shifted to this: "If you jump from here and all the people see angels from God catch your fall, they will surely know you are someone important." The temptation was for Jesus to find his identity in the special power God had given him. "Flaunt your gifts. Show your uniqueness." But Jesus was secure enough in his relationship with his Father that he wasn't dependent on validation from people.

- "Do whatever it takes to be in control." The temptation to power, rooted in pride, is perhaps the greatest weapon in Satan's arsenal. "If you worship me, I will give you everything." The obvious temptation was idolatry, giving the worship reserved for God to another. But the subtle temptation was for Jesus to receive his kingdom by means other than the cross. This was not an option for Jesus, and it elicited his most forceful rebuke of the devil.

Jesus needed no outward sign that God was with him. He didn't need to be the hero. He didn't strive to be in control. All of these were way below his highest calling: to be a Son of his Father.

- Which of these is my current battle? Self-sufficiency, self-importance, or self-agenda?

- How can I gain victory by understanding and living in my position as a child of the Living God?

DIG DEEPER · *EPHESIANS 6:10–18; HEBREWS 1:1–8*

Father, open my eyes to the inheritance you have
given me as a beloved child. Help me not settle for
callings that are below what you have for me. Ground
me in your truth so I may win my battles.

AN UPSIDE-DOWN KINGDOM

DAY 6 — *MATTHEW 5:1–48*

What if everything you've heard about what God wants from you is wrong?

Jesus' first sermon was certainly about a new kind of kingdom, a new way of thinking. But more than that, it revealed the heart of his Father. What must these people have thought when they heard his words? In effect, Jesus was saying:

"You have heard all your life that you should become a better rule follower. But I ask you, what is the state of your heart? How are your relationships with God and with those around you? I tell you that these are the real issues."

He spoke these words with such authority, it was impossible to ignore them. And the one word that starts an avalanche of new thinking is this: *Father.* Seventeen times in Jesus' first recorded sermon he calls God *Father.* Had they ever heard it, even once, used in reference to God before that day? Likely not.

The revolution that Jesus began was fueled by a revelation that God is Father. It will turn our lives upside down too.

This was the one aspect of Jesus' teaching that the religious leaders of his day could not abide by. To them, Yahweh was distant, unapproachable. He could not be known in a personal sense. He was the God of Sinai, of thunder and lightning, speaking to Moses from dark clouds on the mountain. They were forbidden to even speak his name.

Jesus laid the axe to the root of this lie. Through his work on the cross, he would shatter this misconception and begin to rebuild a new perception of God in their minds. The end of following Jesus' teaching is clear: Not to become good rule followers, but *that you may be sons of your Father* (vs 45).

- How different is Jesus' idea of God than the one I have had all my life?

- Are there ways I think about myself in relation to God that must change in order for me to align with Jesus' teaching about God the Father?

DIG DEEPER · *Matthew 6:6–18; 28–33*

Father, help me to see you as you are. I don't want to know you from afar, but as you have revealed yourself through your Son: as a Father. Give me courage to make this change in my thinking.

MORE VALUABLE THAN MY SIN

DAY 7 | *MARK 1:11–15*

Living as a beloved child affects my attitude toward sin. The greatest way to fight temptation is to have a greater love. Our focus should not be on resisting temptation but on being fulfilled in our relationship with our Father.

After hearing the affirmation of his Father and enduring the temptation, Jesus immediately began to preach. His first sermon was simple and clear: "The time is fulfilled, and the kingdom of God is at hand; repent and believe in the gospel." (Mark 1:15)

The fall of man was not so much about acting wrong, but loving wrong. Man turned from loving God toward loving self, pleasure, money, etc. We have never ceased being lovers; we have simply changed the object of our love. If we get love right, our actions will follow.

There are two possible objects of our love, according to John: the Father or the world (1 John 2:15). If we are living in mutual love with our Father, the love of this world will lose its grip. For this reason, morality is secondary and relationship is primary. Love triumphs over law.

Repentance is all about love. God's love for us compels him to call us to repent from the sin that dooms us. Our love for him causes us to drop our sin because we know it breaks his heart and to pursue him because he is supremely better than that sin.

- Have I viewed repentance in a negative or a positive light?

- What would change in my mind and my daily life if I considered repentance as part of the good news, reestablishing my relationship with my Father?

DIG DEEPER · *1 John 2:1–17; Romans 2:4*

Father, how wonderful it is that you draw me with your kindness away from that which harms me and separates me from you. Even more, you draw me into your heart and into the kingdom of your dear Son. Give me grace to respond joyfully and willingly to your great love. Help me to daily repent and believe the gospel.

GOD OF THE DANCE

DAY 8   *JOHN 5:16–30*

Jesus shows us how to be a channel of God's blessing to others. His ministry did not center around his own agenda or his perception of what needed to happen. As beloved children of God, we have the privilege of watching what the Father is doing and joining him in his purpose.

When talking about how the members of the Trinity interrelate, the early church fathers used the term *perichoresis*, which means "circle dance". Their point was that God is a being who lives in community. The Father, Son, and Spirit work together in perfect harmony—in creation, in salvation, in mission. And God has made us in his image as creatures in community.

Just as we are told to keep in step with the Spirit (Galatians 5:16), Jesus kept in step with his Father, mirroring the very heart of God by the work of the Spirit. In him we see the Father: Gracious, compassionate, slow to anger, rich in love. Within the Trinity there is a vibrant, co-working community, with one mind and one purpose.

Our day-to-day relationship with the Father is the source of our ministry to others. We have the Holy Spirit within us—the Spirit of adoption, who cries out, "Abba, Father" (Romans 8:15)—to guide and empower our ministry to others. As daughters and sons, we are invited into this great dance to be co-laborers with him, bringing his kingdom to those around us. What greater privilege could we know?

- How does being a child of my Father change the way I approach my interactions with others today?
- How can I become more aware of what my Father desires to do in the lives of those around me?

DIG DEEPER · *John 12:49–50; 14:9; Ephesians 5:1–2*

Father, what a great privilege you have given me, that I might be invited into your work in those around me today. Help me to be aware of what you are doing and to join in cooperation with you.

LIVING LOVED

DAY 9   *MATTHEW 7:1–29*

Living as a loved person empowers me to love others.

The golden rule is not a legalistic code or good moral advice. It is a way of life that flows from the security and identity of being a beloved child. Out of the assurance that our Father hears our prayers and gives good gifts, we naturally desire to treat others as we would want them to treat us. It is not an "ought to" but a "want to".

As Christ followers, we have the motivation and power to live this way because the Father has treated us as we would want, not as we deserve. We love him because he first loved us. We can love others for the same reason.

The natural, religious mind would have Jesus say, "If you keep my commands, I will love you." What he actually taught was the exact opposite. "If you love me, you will keep my commandments." (John 14:15) We will naturally do the right thing if we love first. Indeed, living in his love is the only thing that gives us the will and the power to obey him.

But Jesus goes further here. He extends his message of "your Father" outward to "your brother". The Father wants the love he lavishes on his children to be poured out through them to others: love one another, do not judge one another, connect to the heart and mission of God through prayer, listen to Jesus' words and act on them.

What makes these words of Jesus so powerful and enduring? He speaks with an authority the people listening had never heard before because his authority flows from relationship with the Father.

- How can my impact increase if I live as a loved child of my Father?
- How can I practically give that kind of love to someone in my life today?

DIG DEEPER · *2 CORINTHIANS 4:11–15; MATTHEW 10:7–8*

God, make me a channel of the love you have given me. Let me increase what you have given me by giving it away to my brothers and sisters today. Make me a good steward of your deep grace.

GOD WHO GIVES IT AWAY

DAY 10   *MATTHEW 10:1–42*

God's children are always being invited into the Father's heart and mission. In a sense, this is what prayer is: a tuning of our hearts to the frequency of the Father.

Jesus never wanted his disciples to merely obey his teaching. He set them on a progression of becoming beloved children. First, he called them to himself and lived life with them, teaching them the ways of the kingdom. After that, he gave them his authority and he sent them out to do the same things he was doing.

Union with Christ means union with his mission. His followers not only carry the same purpose and message, but also literally work with him in his own shared authority. He gives food away, healing away, love away; and he gives his power to his disciples so that the giving can be multiplied through us.

It is possible to walk so closely to Jesus that he will disclose the secrets of his heart. *"Shall I hide from Abraham what I am about to do?"* (Genesis 18:17) We have the privilege of working with God to change the atmosphere around us just as Jesus did. And we do this not only *for* God, but *with* him. He gives us authority to be carriers of his kingdom wherever we go.

Here we see the Father's heart expressed through Jesus. He gives away his authority and power. He sends us to proclaim the good news and to call his covenant people back to him, to stand before kings and in synagogues and, yes, to be flogged for him. The Father will whisper to us and we will shout it from the rooftops.

- What disciplines must I practice to hear my Father's heart?
- Who is he calling me to love and speak truth to today?

DIG DEEPER · *Luke 10:1–9; Genesis 18:17–19*

*Father, it is hard for me to comprehend that I would
be invited into your heart and your mission. Give me
faith that I may walk in your authority and extend your
heart and works to those around me today. Amen.*

GOD OF REST

No doubt, Jesus was a man of action. And he had called his followers and sent them out as men of action to cast out demons, heal the sick, and preach the good news of the kingdom. But he also rested and taught them to rest.

Jesus' life and ministry were a perfect balance of being and doing. Here, when his disciples return, pulsing with the adrenaline rush of ministry, he does not rebuke them saying, "Get back out there! There are still people who do not know the good news yet." No. He says, "Come away with me and rest a while."

Nine times in the book of Luke alone, Jesus retreats to be with his Father. It may surprise us that God himself rested on the seventh day. Why would God rest? Because he was tired? No, he rested because it is part of his very nature. He is a creator, but he is also a rester. And we are made in his image: do-ers and resters. But the fall has alienated us from this rest.

In his mercy, God gifted mankind with a day of the week set apart for the purpose of resting and restoring. Jesus lived a Sabbath lifestyle and taught his disciples to do so. We are not slaves to the Sabbath day; rather, it serves us by giving our bodies rest and our minds and spirits refreshment. It creates space for the grace of God to intersect our lives.

When I practice Sabbath, I tap into the joy of God. I let go of control and trust in his sovereignty. It helps me remember that in Christ I am good enough, worthy enough, loved enough, safe enough…and I can rest.

- Do I find it difficult to make time for rest and recreation in my life?
- Do I find my worth in my accomplishments or in Christ's love for me?

DIG DEEPER · *Mark 2:27; Hebrews 4:1–11*

*God of Rest, you have made me in your image with
the ability to create and to rest. Help me to remember
that I can only be what I need to be for others as I
am resting in you. Teach me that I am valued in your
eyes, that I am loved enough to rest.*

GOD WHO SPEAKS & LISTENS

DAY 12   *Luke 11:1–13*

The disciples saw how important prayer was to Jesus. They couldn't help but notice the difference in his way of praying. We can imagine them saying, "We've seen the Pharisees pray, and we've seen you pray. We like your way better. Lord, teach us to pray. Change our way to your way."

According to Jesus, the starting point of prayer is "Father". A Pharisee never prayed to the Father. His focus was on his own performance. There is more to our walk with God than our own efforts at winning his favor. Jesus gently shifted his disciples' focus toward the generous, active heart of God, their Father. He introduced them to the "how much more" lifestyle of prayer:

- How much more does your Father in heaven want a real relationship?

- How much more does he want to be known for who he is (hallowed)?

- How much more does he want to give us what we need daily?

- How much more does he want to keep our relationships clear of offenses?

- How much more does he want to keep us from evil and lead us in paths of righteousness?

- How much more will he give the Holy Spirit to those who ask?

Prayer is much more than we know it to be. It is an invitation into the heart and mission of God. He wants us with him and he wants us working with him in his purposes on Earth. The heart of prayer leads us into an active, ongoing bond with our Maker.

- What am I specifically asking my Father for today?

- What am I seeking from him?

- What doors is he calling me to knock on?

DIG DEEPER · *Philippians 4:6–7; Ephesians 6:18*

Father, open my heart to know you more, to receive daily what I need from you, to clear my relationships of offense and to walk free from sin. Give me the fullness of your Holy Spirit today and allow me to give it away to others.

GOD TO BE WORSHIPED

DAY 13 | *JOHN 4:1–26*

Think for a moment on the words of Jesus: "You worship what you do not know." He is saying that it is possible to go through the outward motions of worship and not truly know God. So who is this God that we worship? And what is true worship?

God initiates worship by being gracious enough to reveal some of himself to us. When we really see him, we can't help but respond—with our words, our actions, our lives. The result is an ongoing, ever-deepening relationship. This is true worship.

We can't worship big when our understanding of God is small. We can't worship close when we see God as far-off. When we look at major belief systems and their views of God, we find they are very different from what Jesus taught:

- Hindus believe in millions of gods who must be appeased.

- Buddhists say there is no deity.

- Muslims believe in a powerful but detached god.

- New Age practitioners believe they themselves are god.

- Christians believe in a sovereign, almighty God who is also loving and approachable; he is, in fact, a perfect Father.

Can a person connect with God in this life? The answer is yes. Not only can you connect with God, you also can know that you are fully accepted and loved by God through the sacrifice of Jesus Christ. We were created by God to live in relationship with him. And we can worship him freely as our Father—that is good news!

- If I wrote down a list of God's character traits, how many could I list?

- Do I believe God is bigger than my present perception of him? If so, what can I do today to know him better?

DIG DEEPER · *PSALM 96:1–13; COLOSSIANS 1:9–20*

Father, you are infinite and I am finite. There is no way I can know you unless you open my eyes to who you are. I know that there is more to you than I currently understand. Would you show me your character, your ways, your heart? Teach me to respond to who you are and lead me into an ongoing relationship with you through Jesus Christ.

PROUD FATHER

DAY 14   *MARK 9:2–8*

Beside him, the greatest of men cannot stand.

From the heavens resounds a reminder for Jesus and for those around him. The same words that came at his baptism, that prepared him for the temptation, now prepare him for his death. The Father loves, promotes, flaunts his Son.

Do those around him need to be reminded of his Sonship? Yes, of course. They may be enamored with Moses (legalism) or with the prophets (the power and voice of God). But the Son came to fulfill the law and the prophets. He is greater than both, and that is why the Father adds the simple phrase, "listen to him".

I, too, may be measuring my life by how much I know the scriptures, keep the law, or operate in spiritual gifts. Peter wanted to build a shrine to all three men. But the frightening, irresistible voice from the skies narrowed their vision to just one: "Listen to the Son."

If it was important for Jesus to hear the affirming voice of his Father, how much more for you and me? I need to re-remember the good news of adoption every day because my self-talk is the strongest influence in my life. The word *confess* means to "say the same thing as". If my own words to me do not agree with my Father's words about me, I am in trouble. I must allow the Spirit of adoption within me to cry out, "Abba...Father!"

- Am I drawn to following rules or following powerfully gifted people more than to following the Beloved Son of God? In what ways might the Father be recalibrating my vision toward Jesus?

- If I pay attention to how I speak to myself about me, are those words in agreement with what God speaks about me?

DIG DEEPER · *COLOSSIANS 1:15–20; HEBREWS 12:1–3*

*Father, you love your dear Son, and you love me
as a child as well. Let the words of my mouth be
pleasing to you, Lord. Let them agree with what you
are saying. Let me hear the shout of the Spirit in my
heart, crying out to my Father.*

GOD WHO DISCIPLINES

DAY 15   *MATTHEW 11:1–30*

Jesus was not all inspirational quotes and platitudes. Love sometimes requires hard sayings. The correction of his cousin John's understanding of God's plan; the rebuke of the crowds and their unbelief; the judgment that comes to a people when they harden their hearts and do not accept Jesus or his prophets—all of these must be heard.

Our Father is often perplexing to us because he does not fit our expectations. His ways are not our ways and his thoughts not our thoughts. We must guard against the danger of offense. The only way to avoid the quicksand of offense is to understand and live in the reality that we are beloved children.

Jesus shows us the ultimate trust the Father has in the Son: "All things have been handed over to me by my Father." (vs 27) In like manner, sons must trust their Father, for there is a loving heart behind all discipline: *"My son, do not regard lightly the discipline of the Lord, nor be weary when reproved by him. For the Lord disciplines the one he loves, and chastises every son whom he receives."* (Hebrews 12:5–6)

In Scripture we see images of purging and pruning. The threshing floor, the wine press, the refiner's fire—they are all for one thing: to separate the precious from the worthless. God is guiding us into a new place. He is jealous over us, over the image of Jesus in us, over the life he has placed within each of us. He loves us too much to allow us to stay the way we are.

The beauty here is this: Even when we don't understand his ways, we see the arms of the Savior open, inviting us to come, to give him our burdens and learn from him. This is the kind heart of a true Father.

- Am I able to hear and accept hard sayings from my Lord? Do I feel shame or offense when he deals with issues in my life? Do I trust his heart?

- Are there areas of offense that I have given place to in my heart? How can I allow the Holy Spirit to root them out with a revelation of the Father's heart?

DIG DEEPER · *Hebrews 12:5–11; Proverbs 3:11–18*

Father, help me to see that even in seasons of discipline, your goodness and mercy follow me. Show me the subtle areas where I allow offense to enter in and replace that offense with an understanding of your heart and your ways.

GOD MOST HIGH

DAY 16 | *MATTHEW 12:1–50*

Nothing could have prepared me for what I saw in India: Streets full of shops where carved idols sat in the hot sun, waiting to be purchased and taken home where they would be prayed to and brought offerings of food and money. I could not fathom bowing to something that a man had made. Yet I do it all the time.

I often project my earthly understanding and experiences onto God, making him in my own image. In turn, my false perception of God affects my ability to approach him and go deeper with him. It affects my identity, my worth, how I deal with my family, how I minister—basically every aspect of my life. If I get this wrong, I get everything wrong.

The Father relentlessly pursues our hearts by challenging and rearranging our values. Idols, even those that are tied to our religious expression, are the enemy of our walking as beloved children. Jesus actively resists those institutions and idols that prop up our pride:

- There is something greater than the Sabbath—Jesus, the Lord of the Sabbath.

- There is something greater than the temple—Jesus, God incarnate.

- There is something greater than Solomon—Jesus, the wisdom and righteousness of God.

- There is something greater than the prophets—Jesus, the one who was three days and nights in the heart of the earth.

- There is something greater than keeping the law—doing the will of our Father in heaven.

The Father is laser-focused on his Son, for that is what he values most. He will calibrate our values until we share his.

- What idols (images of God that I have created) can I see in my life that rival the True and Living God? In what ways might they be hindering my understanding and walk with him?

- Is there some religious practice or cultural mindset that I have exalted above following Jesus? Do I find my identity and sense of security in this rather than in my relationship with my Father?

DIG DEEPER · *1 John 5:21; 1 Thessalonians 1:8–10*

God Most High, take from my heart the secret
idols that distract me: those things that I look to for
security, provision, protection, and identity instead of
Christ. Remove them by your power and grace and
set my focus on your Son.

MOVED BY COMPASSION

DAY 17   *MATTHEW 14:1–36*

When a wicked king gives a debauched party and responds to a lustful dance with a thoughtless promise, Jesus' cousin is brutally murdered.

How does the heart of a beloved son respond to such an extreme injustice? Jesus withdrew to a private place. We assume this was to grieve, to press into his Father, to get Heaven's perspective, but we don't really know why.

What we do know is that Jesus, who could have been moved by grief to create distance and cut himself off from those who sought him, or by anger to take revenge on the murderous king, did neither of these things.

Instead, he was moved by a different force—compassion. Having gotten the view from his Father's eyes, he struck back at the true enemy. He began to bruise the serpent's head once again; to heal the sick, to feed the hungry, to preach the good news to the poor. Over and over in the gospels we see this response from Jesus. He allows compassion to overcome all other emotions and drive his response.

Union with the Father will reset the son and daughter to Heaven's perspective. It will free us from the chains of offense and release us to refocus on our calling.

- Am I characterized by allowing compassion to overpower other emotions as I respond to those around me?

- How can I yield to the Spirit's work of bearing the fruit of love and self-control in me today?

DIG DEEPER · *1 Peter 3:8–9; Psalm 34:11–15*

*Grant me, Lord, the ability to be moved with
compassion, not distracted by the actions of orphans.
Let me see the true enemy and fight him with grace
and power in your name.*

GOD THE JUST

DAY 18   *MATTHEW 20:1–34*

God has a right to do what he wants with what is his. And sometimes the Father's justice seems contrary to our sense of fairness.

In this chapter and the one before it, Jesus deals with many different types of people: working class, wealthy, religious leaders, little children, close friends. Being in tune with his Father allowed Jesus to respond correctly to every situation, though each response needed to be different. When we are not sure how to respond to those around us, it helps to ask the most important question: *What does love look like in this situation?*

Some received what they asked for in this chapter and some did not. Some received what they did not deserve. And some did not receive what they felt entitled to. The disciples were denied their mother's request. The blind men received theirs. Jesus asked them both the same question: "What do you want me to do for you?" And all of them still followed him.

The Father knows his purposes and isn't obligated to reveal them to us. Often he does, but just as often he knows we are not in a position to grasp them. Only in abiding can we sense his heart and respond correctly. Otherwise we will be offended, and we will fight against Heaven's agenda.

Jesus had to die cruelly and unjustly. The sons of Zebedee had to drink the same cup. And we must drink the cup set before us. Ironically, and beautifully, the Father gives us the power needed to surrender to his wise and good will.

- Are there offenses in my heart toward God's actions or inactions? What would surrender look like in those situations?
- What does love look like in the context of those I will walk with today?

DIG DEEPER · *Matthew 11:6; John 16:12–15*

*God of Justice, give me wisdom to take each person
as they are today, to discern what love looks like in
each situation. Deliver me from offense and empower
me to surrender to your good justice.*

GOD OF KINDNESS & SEVERITY

DAY 19   *Mark 2:1–3:35*

Jesus shows us a Father who is willing to heal, to forgive sins, to eat with sinners, and to invite the cultural enemy into his inner circle. He draws in those whom society has pushed away. He is remarkably open, accessible, and welcoming.

And yet he is constantly at odds with those who misrepresent him. He resists the teachers of his own law because they disregarded the spirit of the law in order to keep the letter of the law. They were afraid Jesus would upset their status, touch their traditions, reduce their power.

The Father gives grace to the humble but resists the proud. And those proud ones do most ferociously resist him. They look for ways to trap Jesus, to bring him down. They see with their own eyes the Lord's compassion and then promptly turn to kill him. They align themselves with a godless nation—their mortal enemy, Rome—to accomplish what their father, the devil, wants. And in the end, God resists them. Their pride goes before their own destruction.

Remarkably, the religious leaders attribute Jesus' works to the devil, and yet the very demons see him as the Son of God. An orphan heart causes one to get things perfectly, precisely wrong.

- Have I seen God as one who is tender to those in the margins? Is my heart for those on the outside the same as his?

- Do I carry the same zeal as Jesus against those who misrepresent God?

DIG DEEPER · *Romans 11:22–24; 1 Peter 5:5–7*

*God of Kindness, mold my heart until it holds
compassion for those who are needy and outcast.
God of Severity, help me to stand against all that
misrepresents you and to be an agent of truth where
you put me today.*

HOW ORPHANS LIVE

DAY 20   *MATTHEW 23:1–39*

The scribes and Pharisees seemed righteous, but they attempted to be clean from the outside in. They were known in their day as God's representatives, but they had bad genes. Jesus called them children of hell: "*You are of your father the Devil.*" (John 8:44)

The Son of God speaks to those who claim Abraham as their father. They were children of the law, but they didn't know God. They were proud of their heritage, but they were orphans. There was no heavenly DNA in them, no trace of the Father's image. And Jesus reserves his most scathing words for them.

Here we see how orphans live:

- Hypocrisy: They do not live out what they teach.

- Oppression: They lay heavy burdens on others that they themselves will not carry.

- Fear of man: They live to impress others, and they love titles.

- Religious pride: They box up the word of God and wear it in order to bring honor to themselves.

- Deception: They do not keep their oaths.

- Legalism, not love: They work hard to keep the smallest rule but do not care for people.

- Concern for outward appearances: They take care to look beautiful on the outside, but they are rotten within.

This is the best that continuing to live under the law can do for you. What worse indictment could come from the lips of the Son of God than, "How are you to escape being sentenced to hell?"

The Father longs for us to carry his DNA, but this cannot happen from the outside in—it must begin with regeneration. We must be born again.

- What areas of self-righteousness am I trusting in?
- Am I striving in my own power to become what I already am in Christ?

DIG DEEPER · *ROMANS 10:1–4; PROVERBS 14:12*

*Father of the Fatherless, thank you that through
the work of Jesus I am born again, remade in your
image. Take me deeper in an understanding of your
ways. Help me to live from the core of who you have
made me: from the DNA of Heaven. Let others see
your image in me today.*

GOD OF OPEN ARMS

DAY 21 | *MATTHEW 11:25–30*

Scowling and cross-armed, threatening and distant—this is the way mankind has viewed their gods through the ages. Despots who demand to be appeased and are never satisfied. What a different picture Jesus shows us.

There is no shame in weariness. Instead, there is a welcome entry into his presence and his heart. Our God grants access: "Come to me, all who labor and are heavy laden, and I will give you rest." The Father stands with open arms, and he holds for us the thing we need most: He invites us to lean in, to rest, to breathe, to dream again.

Jesus offers a great exchange. Not only does he offer his righteousness for our sin, but he also offers to take the burdens we are bearing and give us a different yoke. And in that process he offers wisdom, turning our crisis into a teachable moment. In the midst of the weariness, he opens to us his meek, humble, open heart.

Those who need justice, let them come and receive it. Let the children come and do not forbid them. Let the unworthy tax collector and sinner come. Let the blind man come and receive his sight.

It is good when we find ourselves bankrupt, for that is a prerequisite to being received by Christ. Jesus is the champion of all those in the margins. He is our champion. When we feel the lowest, the weakest, the most unworthy, his arms are wide open to us, inviting us in to receive everything we need.

- When I lift my eyes to Heaven, do I see the arms of my Savior open and beckoning me to come?

- What burdens am I currently bearing that his strong arms are ready to take from me? What easy yoke is he offering?

DIG DEEPER · *Psalm 68:19–20; 1 Peter 5:6–7*

God of Open Arms, I see you standing, beckoning,
welcoming me into your care. Teach me to lay aside
the weights, shed the hindrances, and run to you
each day, with each care. Teach me your ways as I
learn to live in your rest.

GOD OF THE HEART

DAY 22   *MARK 7:1–30*

The Father doesn't want rule followers; he wants lovers. Relationship is the top priority, and laws and traditions can be the enemies of love. When the Pharisees and teachers of the law journeyed from Jerusalem and gathered around Jesus, the first thing they addressed were their rules.

They may have known the scriptures, but their traditions had trumped God's commands. They had developed a type of obsessive compulsive disorder—a state of mental instability—concerning their washings and man-made rituals. Their rules were ruling their lives. And they could not tolerate anyone who didn't agree with their convictions.

The proud leaders regarded their way of doing things above their love for God and their love for people. They were imposters, pretending to love God when they loved their own superiority and religious regimen. Jesus wanted to establish a different rule.

The way of the Father is not "keep my rules", but "open your hearts". His emphasis is on the heart because the heart affects everything we do. Jesus was unimpressed with proud religious leaders. But he was very impressed with a desperate foreign woman who approached him on the basis of faith and love.

- Am I more in love with God or my own idea of what it means to follow God?

- Are there areas in which I need to transition from law to love? Is my heart soft enough to be corrected?

DIG DEEPER · *Matthew 15:16–20; Proverbs 4:23*

Father, thank you that serving you is more than outward rituals and duty. I marvel that you are interested in a relationship with me—that you want the very heart of me to know who you are. By the power of your Spirit, move me from duty to devotion, from law to love.

GOD OF LEGACY

DAY 23   *MATTHEW 19:23–30*

Peter poses the question in the back of all our minds: "We have left all to follow you…what do we get out of it?" Jesus' response: "Whatever you lose for my name's sake will be rewarded."

When Jesus uses the words "for my name's sake", he is speaking of legacy. Legacy is something handed to us from the past and then handed on into the future. All that God does is connected to his name, and that name is connected to his purpose and his honor.

Legacy is what God does for us because of who he is (to protect his name). It is also what we do for him because of who he is (to promote his name).

I share a name with my deceased grandfather. Now I am the patriarch of our family, and my grandson shares that same name. It is an honor to have someone named after you—like a tribute in human form. But it is also a responsibility. What will I do to uphold the honor of my Father's Name?

It is possible to live for the sake of my own reputation. But God honors those who have a mind for *his* legacy, for *his* name's sake. Authority, presence, power, healing, teaching, baptizing, transforming lives—this was to be the fruit of the disciple who was obeying Christ and moving on to maturity.

If I am to be like Christ, I must be reproducing myself in others—for his name's sake.

This is why we make disciples. We cannot follow Jesus without doing so.

- How much of my walk with God is concerned with what I get from him rather than what he gets from me?

- What changes in perspective would come if I viewed each day as an opportunity to honor and spread the name of Jesus?

DIG DEEPER · *Psalm 79:8–9; Isaiah 48:9–11*

God of Legacy, you have saved me and drawn me
to yourself for your name's sake. Help me to be more
concerned with what you get from me than what I
get from you. Refocus me today and empower me to
live for your name's sake.

GOD OF PURPOSE

DAY 24 | *JOHN 15:1–27*

God is not detached or passive. Rather, he is ever-active, ever-moving toward a purpose—in us and in the world.

The Father washes us, prunes us, causes us to be fruitful as we live in Christ. Pruning comes to all of us, but it is important to understand that his pruning is not punishment. It is always kind and purposeful. The pruning process is not designed to kill you but to cut away that which is killing you—to make you more alive. The process is for your good…and for his glory.

Over and over these words flow from Jesus' lips here: Father…abide…love…fruit. He shows us a circle of relationship which is not characterized by law-keeping but by life-living. We glorify him as we bear much fruit. We grow from servants to friends. We begin to know his heart more so that we want the things he wants, and therefore our prayers are more effective and are answered consistently.

Prayer, as Jesus presents it here, is not God saying to us, "Your wish is my command." Rather, as we mature in him, his command becomes our wish.

Abiding and being formed in his purpose are foreshadows of the lives his disciples must live—and the deaths they must die. "They will treat you as they treat me; hate you as they hate me." The greatest love is to lay down your life. And from this, the greatest fruit is born.

- What life-robbing things might the Father be pruning from my life today?

- Does the thought of losing these things bring me panic, or relief?

DIG DEEPER · *JOHN 12:23–26; PSALM 1:1–6*

God of Purpose, draw me into a deeper experience of abiding in you. Cut away those things that are sapping the life from me and cause your heart to be pressed into my own. Conform me to yourself until my prayers are your prayers, my purpose your purpose.

GOD OF MY DARKEST DAYS

DAY 25   *JOHN 17:1–26*

On the eve of his most horribly traumatic day, knowing the suffering that was just hours away—the weight of the world, the sin of the world, the prospect of separation from the Father, extreme psychological duress, and the dread of the crucifixion—still Jesus pressed into his relationship with the Father through prayer.

What does this prayer reveal to us? On his darkest day, the first word out of Jesus' mouth was "Father". His default mode was to pray a prayer of intimacy, recalling relationship that had been from the beginning. He lifted his eyes to a trustworthy Father, one who could be confided in, who was on his side, and who would glorify him to the world—even in this darkest hour.

His words recalled the history of their love: "I have known you. You gave me authority. We share all things freely. I know the love you have for me. You gave me words, I spoke them. You gave me men, I kept them. I am coming back to you. Now, glorify me with the glory we shared before the world began."

Jesus wasn't lost in his own despair. He grounded himself in the truth of his relationship and was able to turn his prayers outward toward his disciples—and toward us.

"I do not ask for these only, but also for those who will believe in me through their word." He prayed for our joy, protection, and sanctification. He prayed for unity with each other and with himself and his Father. This is the type of prayer that only flows out of relationship—even on our darkest day.

- What is my normal response when I am in despair? Do I shrink back like an orphan or press in like a beloved child?

- What Scripture or revelation of God's character can I default to that will change my perspective?

DIG DEEPER · *PSALM 3:1–8; 2 TIMOTHY 3:10–17*

God of My Darkest Days, you have always been faithful to me. You bless me when I do not deserve it. You provide for my every need. You are near when I am in despair. Your voice strengthens me even there. May our relationship grow until I can instinctively rest in your love, even in the crucible.

GOD WHO SPEAKS

DAY 26 — *JOHN 1:1–51*

Silent fathers are perhaps the hardest to live with because you never know where you stand. You never really know what they are like or what they think of you.

God our Father is not silent—he has spoken through Jesus. John's entire focus is that we might believe that Jesus is the Son of God: This is why he tells us so much about Jesus in the first chapter of his gospel.

Jesus has always been ("in the beginning"). Jesus is distinct from God the Father ("the Word was with God"). Yet, Jesus was one with the Father ("the Word was God"). Jesus was a flesh and blood human being ("the Word was made flesh"). He is full of grace and full of truth.

The people John introduces in this chapter give Jesus seven titles:

- The Lamb of God who takes away our sin—John the Baptizer

- Son of God—John the Baptizer

- Teacher—John's disciples

- Messiah—Andrew

- Jesus of Nazareth—Philip

- King of Israel—Nathaniel

- Son of Man—Jesus himself

Through these titles, John spells out the importance of this man, Jesus. This fully human Jesus, from an insignificant town called Nazareth, is Israel's long-awaited Messiah, king, and teacher, and the Son of God who will die for the sins of the world. There is no greater claim to make about someone.

But more than that, he is the voice, the heart, the very expression of the Father. Because the Father wants to be known. He is not silent…but are we listening?

- God has spoken to every generation and every people group through his Son, Jesus. He also speaks to us personally through him. What do you sense he is speaking to you today?

DIG DEEPER · *1 John 5:1–5; John 20:30–31*

Father Who Speaks, I thank you that you have not left me wondering about who you are and what you think about me. I am grateful that you reveal yourself through your Son Jesus and that you offer me eternal life through him. Please continue to speak to me through your Son.

GOD ALL WISE

DAY 27   *JOHN 3:1–36*

In one of the most well-known passages of the Bible, Jesus both tells of God's love and provision for sinners and tells us the truth of judgment and wrath that abides upon unbelievers. If we understand both the holiness of God and the love of God, we must wrestle with the tension these two truths hold.

There is a problem with forgiveness. How can God remain true to his holiness and his love without compromising either? In order to maintain his integrity and retain his character, he must judge the sinners he loves…and he must love those who deserve judgment.

The problem is this: The way God chooses to forgive sinners and reconcile them to himself must be consistent with his character. Man owes something to God, and yet man cannot pay it—only the God-man can. The All-Wise God solved this enigma in the cross of Christ.

At the cross, inflexible righteousness clashed with infinite love. The Father does not compromise his holiness to spare or spoil us. He does not compromise his love in order to crush us under his holy wrath. He can save us and remain true to his unchanging, loving, holy nature only by substituting himself for us.

At the cross, God through Christ paid the full penalty of our disobedience himself. He bore the judgment we deserve in order to bring us the forgiveness we don't deserve. His "holy love" was satisfied.

Sin is man substituting himself for God. Salvation is God substituting himself for man. The cross is the solution to the problem of our sin and reconciles us to a holy and loving God. *"Oh, the depth of the riches both of the wisdom and knowledge of God! How unsearchable are his judgments and his ways past finding out!"* (Romans 11:33, NKJV)

- Why can't God just forgive us without the cross of Christ? Why would "overlooking" our sin compromise his character?

- How might my personal sacrifice solve relational problems among those around me?

DIG DEEPER · *ROMANS 11:33–36; 1 CORINTHIANS 1:18–25*

God All Wise, how marvelous is the wisdom you have shown in solving the dilemma that doomed my soul. What a beautiful mystery you have invited me into, that I can be reconciled to all that you are through the sacrifice of Jesus Christ. Help me to be ever enthralled by the beauty of the cross.

GOD WHO HONORS OBEDIENCE

DAY 28   *MATTHEW 27:1–66*

They rise early, the orphan-hearted, to plot and to force their plans. These religious leaders who researched and revered the texts that spoke of the Messiah were hell-bent on silencing him. The orphan-hearted cover their wickedness with a righteous veneer, but in the end they despair under the weight of their own decisions until they destroy themselves. This is the way of an orphan.

True sons do not feel the need to justify themselves. "Are you the king of the Jews?" Yes, and more than a king. Even the rugged Roman centurion saw it, terrified and convinced: "Truly this was the Son of God!"

Yet the familiar phrase comes again from the Accuser through his mockers: "If you are the Son of God, come down from the cross." As in the wilderness, Jesus hears again the questioning of his sonship and the temptation to come into his glory without the cross.

A son submits to his Father. An orphan denies, runs, scrambles to save his own kingdom. For the orphans, the great miracle would have been coming down from the cross, escaping the suffering. But the greater miracle was staying on the cross.

For if he did not endure the cross, he would never have been resurrected. And his obedience was not merely for his Father; it was for us. The veil is torn; holiness floods out; dead people spring to life again; witness is borne to others. Life floods the world.

- Are there areas of my life where I am holding on to my own kingdom, looking for an easy way rather than the Father's way?

- What would it take to practically submit to the Father's better plan? What needs to change in my mind and actions today?

DIG DEEPER · *Matthew 16:21–25; Hebrews 12:1–3*

Father, I know you honor obedience, and I believe that your way is better than mine. Let me lay back into your love and wisdom and trust you more, though all around me is raging.

GOD WHO RAISES THE DEAD

DAY 29   *ACTS 13:28–39*

Here we see the total commitment of the Father's love for his Son. After Jesus had obeyed fully, even to death on the cross, his Father would not allow this kind of love to end in corruption. God raised him from the dead in power, and through his life all things are made new.

The resurrection is not just a historical event. It is an event that breaks into history with the power of another world. It is not merely a creed, but a life-altering truth. It is one thing to believe in the doctrine of the resurrection. It is another thing altogether to meet this person who was raised from the dead.

What does the Resurrection of Christ mean to me today? It is the Father's validation of all that Jesus Christ said about Himself. It means I can be forgiven and have a brand new life. It means the living Christ is present and active in my life today, and it ensures that I will be resurrected also (1 Corinthians 15:20–23).

The Father loved his Son by raising him up. And through that resurrection he made us sons and daughters and gave us a living hope. This is what elevates Christianity above the world of "religious ideas" and into the realm of life-changing relationship with the living God.

- How do I see the love of the Father for his Son and for me through the resurrection?

- What kind of victory does the resurrection reveal? How does that victory show itself in my life?

DIG DEEPER · *1 CORINTHIANS 15:12–26; PHILIPPIANS 2:4–11*

God Who Raises the Dead, I thank you for your amazing plan of salvation. When I was dead in my sins, you sent Jesus to die in my place and you raised him up in power. Now, through his life you have also raised me up together with him. Thank you for the everlasting life you have given me in Jesus.

THE FATHER WHO LOVES A FULL HOUSE

DAY 30 | *LUKE 14:12–35*

The Father loves a party. And he wants everyone to be there. *"Go out to the roads and country lanes and compel them to come in, so that my house will be full."* (vs 23, NIV)

Whatever it takes, he will populate his banquet. If those first invited make excuses, he will extend the invitation to others. The context indicates that the religious Jewish leaders who rejected him would miss out on the banquet. Yet in his mercy he welcomes even we who are in the country lanes of history.

The heart of the Father beats strongly in Jesus. The sick, the poor, the crippled and blind—all those who could never repay him—he invites. He counted the cost to bring the likes of us to the banquet. He took the low place, gave up his rights, emptied himself and gave everything, as he calls us to do. All of this because the Father's heart is extravagant, lavishing his love through an eternal banquet, giving everything for the joy of our presence.

Jesus never demanded anything from us that he did not perfectly live out in his incarnation. May the heart of Jesus beat strongly in us. May our eyes be opened to those in the margins around us. And may we invite everyone to the party.

- Who around me today is the Father inviting to his banquet?
- How can I extend an invitation?

DIG DEEPER · *Philippians 2:4–11; Matthew 28:18–20*

*Father, I know that you love a full house. You have
paid everything, set the tables, and sent out the call.
I accept your invitation, and I want to be your
messenger to carry that invitation to others today.*

IRRESISTIBLE JESUS

WHY THE DISCIPLES LEFT ALL TO FOLLOW HIM...
AND WHY WE SHOULD TOO

BOOK TWO

INTRODUCTION

Years ago the Holy Spirit impressed me to study the life of Jesus in order to see just what it was about him that caused his disciples to give their lives in absolute commitment to him and to his message. I began a study through the gospels, making notes on what they would have seen and heard that would have compelled them so strongly.

What was it about this man that convinced them that he was indeed God, indeed the Messiah that was promised, indeed the king of an unseen and heavenly kingdom, and worth losing all to follow?

After years of looking afresh at the life of Jesus Christ, I marvel more deeply than ever over him—his character, his words, and his works. There has never been a man to compare with Jesus Christ. He is to be admired above all other men, even if he weren't the Only Begotten Son of God, the Lord of the Universe. As I see him, I long to be like him, to serve him, to be one with him. The closer I get to him, the more beautiful he is.

Through this study, I hope to show you even a sliver of the beauty and compassion and grandeur I have discovered while dwelling on the life of our Savior, our irresistible Jesus.

DAILY READINGS

IRRESISTIBLE MAGNETISM

DAY 1   *MATTHEW 4:18–25*

We all know that person who always seems to be the center of things—the life of the party. We love to be around them, to draw from their energy…but we would probably never sell everything to follow them wherever they lead.

Jesus Christ had irresistible magnetism. There was something about him that caused people to pause and see his uniqueness, something that demanded a response. One minute they were casting or mending a net or collecting a tax, and the next they were off, risking all that was familiar to them to follow this teacher into the unknown.

But what could have enticed them to leave everything? What were they looking for? An escape to a life of adventure? A desire for power or fame or to see miracles? A cabinet post in the Messiah's kingdom?

And what did they find when they followed? A kingdom, all right, but not what they expected. Adventure, sure, but not at all what they imagined. It was more of a cross than a crown they found. Were they being led by a Messiah or a martyr?

The words, the miracles, the kingdom he spoke of: All of it was enticing. And there was surely something about Jesus' personality and character that seemed worthy of honor. But it was more than that. It was a calling, not from a man but from the Almighty. They couldn't have known for sure that he was the Messiah when they started out. They took a journey of faith.

Some people only need a nudge to leave all and follow a dream. Others are more rooted and must count the cost more carefully. Regardless of our tendency, Jesus extends the same invitation to us all—and it is an invitation to a person, not a movement—"Follow me."

- When I reflect on those moments when Christ nudged me onto a path of discipleship, what was it about him that drew me to him?

- What did I find about him that was unexpected?

DIG DEEPER · *JOHN 1:35–51; LUKE 18:28–30*

Father, I see in your Son an extraordinary man.
A man of wisdom, power, and kindness. I see in him
what I have not found in any other human, and I thirst
to know more. Open my eyes to see his humanity and his
deity clearer and to follow him nearer.

THE PROPHETIC WITNESS OF JESUS

DAY 2   *JOHN 5:1–47*

Jesus was born into the context of a covenant people and covenant promises. There is an astounding amount of prophetic witness from ancient Scripture about who Jesus is. In fact, his entire life, death, and resurrection were foretold hundreds of years before he lived on Earth. He was the culmination of centuries of predictions and expectancy.

In this passage, Jesus is brought to trial by religious leaders who are consumed with zeal to convict him. But the figurative courtroom is packed with witnesses *for* him. John tells of these witnesses throughout his gospel.

The first witness called is John the Baptizer, the forerunner (5:32–33), followed by the voice of the Father himself at Jesus' baptism (5:37). Then Moses and the prophets take the stand (5:45–46). Jesus' own words testify of him (8:14), and the works he did bear witness (10:25). Finally, the Holy Spirit gives a compelling testimony (15:26), and Jesus' own followers tell what they have seen and heard (15:27).

But the star witnesses are the scriptures. Jesus has always been found there. The Torah that the disciples were taught from youth, that the Pharisees studied and prided themselves in knowing, points to him: *"You search the Scriptures because you think that in them you have eternal life; and it is they that bear witness about me."* (5:39)

Jesus made the scriptures come alive to his followers because they saw him in them. He still does this today.

- How have each of the witnesses discussed above spoken directly to my life?

- How can my life bear witness to Jesus today?

DIG DEEPER · *LUKE 24:25–27; 1 CORINTHIANS 15:1–6*

Father, I am overwhelmed when I think of the centuries of prophecy and the faithful followers who have witnessed about who Jesus is through the ages. Help me to continually grow in my knowledge and wonder of Jesus, and empower me to hold him out to those around me today.

BORN FROM ABOVE

DAY 3   *JOHN 1:1–18*

Jesus was not received by everyone, but those who did receive him got much more than they bargained for. Surely his disciples recognized his uniqueness. John saw him as the very Word of God living among them. The one who was full of life and light and grace and truth had come into their world and was changing everything. But something more was happening: They began to recognize those qualities within themselves.

As they received him, God was giving them power to become sons of God in their own right. As Ezekiel had foretold, their old hearts of stone were taken away, and God was giving them new hearts of flesh (Ezekiel 11:19; 36:26). He was putting his Spirit in them and causing them to follow him. This was the New Covenant, the new life—this was being "born of the Spirit" (John 3:5–8).

When this happens to a person, there is no denying it. It comes from God. It is not an outside-in moral resolution, but rather an inside-out supernatural revolution. This was not happening by an act of the flesh but by the Spirit of God. Everything was different—old things were passing away, and all things were becoming new.

Perhaps the greatest convincing came as they realized this new birth was actually alive in them. They found themselves to be children of God, and this new life led them to new places and new experiences, and to sharing this good news with others.

- Have I experienced this new life that Christ offers? Can I recollect what my life was like before I was born again?

- How is becoming a new creation different from "turning over a new leaf"?

DIG DEEPER · *2 Corinthians 5:17–21; Ezekiel 36:22–28*

Father, what a promise you have given to us that we are not stuck in our sin, but you have made a way into a new life in Christ. It's so wonderful that our relationship with you is not merely a moral obligation, but your very Spirit is inside us, causing us to follow you. Thank you for this gift of grace.

BREAD & CIRCUSES

DAY 4 | *JOHN 6:1–53*

Things were picking up. After ministry in rural towns to relatively small crowds, the word had spread. As momentum continued to build, people followed Jesus by the thousands. But they didn't follow him for who he was. They followed him because of what he did for them.

Sometimes in their haste, the crowds set out without enough provisions. Jesus saw them and was moved by compassion, so he performed another miracle, this time feeding them in the wilderness with a few loaves and fishes. Just like God fed Israel in the wilderness through the miracle of manna, the Bread of Life was sustaining them. This would have been a great opportunity for Jesus to solidify his support, to grow his ministry by the use of his powers. As they kept receiving from his hand, they wanted to make him king.

But Jesus would have none of it. His response was contrary to the common practice of the day from those in power. The Roman poet Juvenal, who lived a generation after Jesus, referred to Roman laws that were passed specifically to keep the allegiance of poorer voters. Those in power promised "bread and circuses" to keep the voters happy and well-behaved (Juvenal, *Satires* 10.81). "Feed and entertain the masses so you can keep power"—that was the strategy.

Jesus did the exact opposite. Instead of telling the crowds what he would give them, he told them what he demanded from them: total commitment. The call was clear, but hard to hear: "I am the living bread that came down from heaven.... Truly, truly, I say to you, unless you eat the flesh of the Son of Man and drink his blood, you have no life in you." (6:51, 53)

Staggered as they were by Jesus' statements, the disciples understood that he was not playing games. He did not pander for political power. Perhaps this is how they knew he was the real deal.

- Do I follow Jesus only because of the benefits that come my way? Do I seek God's hand instead of his face?

- Do I shy away from his demands to commit completely to him?

DIG DEEPER · *Matthew 22:15–22; John 18:28–40*

Father, I am grateful that Jesus held true to the message that you wanted him to speak and that we needed to hear. He was not swayed by success nor did he cater to the crowds. Help me submit to his message and resist my tendency to follow him only because he meets my needs.

GRACE & TRUTH

DAY 5   *JOHN 4:1–30*

Technically, he did not *have* to go through Samaria. Any respectable Jew would have taken the route around Samaria, though it added miles to his journey. He did not *have* to speak to a woman. He should not have, according to his culture and customs—especially *this* woman.

But in a sense, he *did* have to do these things, for his Father had a task for him. His Father's leading took him there. Kindness for the outcast, despised, half-breed Samaritans took him there. Compassion overcame racism and historical feuds. Grace overcame taboos and gender gaps. He did what he saw his Father doing.

But in his mercy he never compromised truth. The law came by Moses, John tells us, but Jesus perfectly wedded grace with truth. When he spoke to the woman at the well, he heard the voice of the Spirit, and he put his finger directly on what the Spirit revealed. He dealt with her specific sins and wrong religious narratives, and he called her to repentance—the only thing that brings life. Even more, he opened her eyes to her highest calling as a daughter and worshiper of Yahweh.

He made himself vulnerable—the Living Water was thirsty. He took a risk. He did not get sidetracked. He loved enough to speak the truth. And he did all of this as his disciples looked on and marveled. This man lived comfortably, perfectly, in the tension of grace and truth.

- How might the grace and truth of Jesus be breaking into my life to deal with specific sins and wrong thinking in me?

- How can I allow this grace and truth to flow through me to others today?

DIG DEEPER · *JOHN 1:14–17; COLOSSIANS 1:3–8*

Father, the life-giving grace of Jesus is staggering.
The fact that he tells me the truth and yet invites me into
a relationship with you amazes me and makes me desire
you more and more. Help me grow in this grace and
truth and hold it out to others.

THE TEACHER

No one had ever taught like this man. It was not just the words he spoke, but the authority he spoke them with. And not just the authority, but the change those words initiated. Jesus was introducing the culture of another kingdom to the earth.

Jesus was explaining the culture of Heaven to an earthbound humanity. A culture is the beliefs of a people and the way those beliefs are lived out in daily life. It is "the way we do things around here."

Not a single teaching or interaction went by without something that seemed upside down to the hearers: The last would be first; the greatest of all is the one who serves all; the inside is more important than the outside; our hope is in God's righteousness, not our own.

Jesus thoroughly knew the Old Testament scriptures, and he interpreted them correctly. He was a man of deep wisdom who understood the heart and purposes of God, and he freely shared these with his followers. He was uncommonly clever and caught the people who tried to trick him in their own traps. He shut the mouths of those who opposed him.

But his motivation wasn't to outsmart others. He called his followers to a higher way of living—to live life more abundantly. Love your Maker, love your neighbor. Have faith in God. Relax and learn to trust your Father for all your needs. This was the message that drew many to love and follow him and many others to hate him fiercely.

- In what ways have I found the teachings of Jesus to be "upside down"?
- What particular point of my culture (the way I believe and live my life) is Jesus challenging today?

DIG DEEPER · *PSALM 19:7–14; LUKE 4:14–22*

Father, I marvel at the world that Jesus has revealed to us through his wise teaching. Help me to understand what your kingdom is like and to let go of the things from my culture that hold me back from living in your ways. May the words of the Great Teacher reshape my life.

HARD SAYINGS

DAY 7   *JOHN 6:50–71*

Words of wisdom and hope—these characterized Jesus' teachings. But he did not curry favor with his words. Never once.

From a motivation of love, he sometimes spoke things that were hard to hear. The first word of his first recorded message was, "Repent." He called his followers to change. Our tendency may be to say nothing that will alienate others, but there is something refreshing about someone who will speak plain truth.

"*Let the dead bury their dead…*" "*Sell all that you have…*" "*If your right eye offends you, pluck it out…*" The list goes on. Jesus clearly taught things that demanded a response. He called his followers to radical commitment, and to truly hear him was to know that indifference was not an option. "*Whoever is not with me is against me.*" (Matthew 8:22; Luke 18:22; Matthew 18:9; 12:30)

It has been said that Jesus comforts the afflicted and afflicts the comfortable. This was true in first-century Palestine and continues to be so for us today. Many will enthusiastically embrace some of his teachings while ignoring others. His early followers felt the tension: "On hearing it, many of his disciples said, 'This is a hard teaching. Who can accept it?'" (John 6:60)

It is true that these hard sayings must be heard within their historical and literary context, but there is no denying the tension his words bring. Our reaction might have been, *Jesus, don't bring those things up. Who will follow you if you keep talking like that?* But the truth is this: True disciples will follow him because they know he loves them enough to tell them the truth.

- What parts of Jesus' teaching bring me comfort? What parts would I rather skip over?

- Am I courageous enough to ask the Father to help me face and follow the hard teachings of Jesus?

DIG DEEPER · *Matthew 10:34–39; 12:22–37*

Father, I thank you that we do not have to grope for truth. Your Son himself is truth and he made truth known to us. Your Spirit guides us into all truth. I believe Jesus has the words of life. Fill me with courage to hear and do even his hard sayings.

THE GOD WHO STOOPS

DAY 8   *JOHN 13:1–38*

It was just before the Passover Feast commemorating the blood of the Lamb which held off the judgment of God. Jesus, the Lamb of God, had been inspected by the priests and political leaders of his day. No fault was found in him; he was a fitting sacrifice. He was ready to step into his destiny to fulfill all that the Feast represented. This was the crescendo of all eternity—and what was on his mind?

Where is that towel?

While the disciples were ready to fight for a place by the throne, they would not fight for a towel. It never even crossed their minds. Yet, the God of glory stooped down to wash their feet. How could Jesus, on the verge of this awful moment, be present and mindful enough to do such an unexpected thing? Because he understood that God had given him power over all things. He knew where he came from, and he knew where he was going. He was secure enough to stoop, to wash, to serve. He even washed the feet of the one who would betray him.

In Psalm 113, David reveals a stunning fact: Almighty God humbles himself even to behold Heaven. Yet, though he is high, he stoops down to lift the poor and needy (vs 7). David had experienced this personally. Jesus revealed this attribute of the Father's character through wonders and compassion. Blind, lame, lepers, poor, deaf, dead—God stoops down from Heaven through Jesus to all of these and meets them at their point of pain.

Hours before his crucifixion, Jesus was calming and reassuring those he loved. Being like God is not climbing up the ladder of success, but stooping down to lift others, bringing hope to people in the margins.

- Imagine for a moment, a being with unlimited power who is bent on evil. Now imagine this same being moved instead by compassion, bent on lifting up the lowly. Imagine him giving us the power to do the same.

- In what ways can I walk in Jesus' footsteps to lift the lowly today?

DIG DEEPER · *2 Corinthians 8:9; Philippians 2:1–11*

Father, like David, I am amazed that although you are enthroned on high, yet you humble yourself to lift up the poor. There is no other god like you, who loves with a self-emptying, initiating love that is centered on others. Mold me into the kind of person who reaches into the margins and helps the helpless in your name.

WHEN GOD SPOKE FROM HEAVEN

DAY 9 · *LUKE 9:18–36*

Jesus' disciples were convinced that the scriptures spoke of him. They heard the declaration of John the Baptist that he was the Lamb of God. They heard Jesus' own teachings, full of authority and wisdom and love. But hearing the voice of God from Heaven was another thing altogether.

The three who went with Jesus to the mountaintop had no frame of reference for what was about to happen to them. How could they? For who ever dreamt of seeing such things?

First, the Son of Man took on a glory that was other-worldly—the glory of Heaven, his true nature—before their eyes. Peter had just confessed his belief that Jesus was the Messiah, but this was not on his grid. That day he learned that Jesus is always more than our current revelation of him.

On top of that, Moses and Elijah, the two greatest heroes of these men's faith, appeared with Jesus. The great law-giver and the most revered prophet stood together with their Rabbi, speaking to him about what he was to accomplish in Jerusalem. Could it be that what Jesus would do was greater than the law and prophets?

This experience alone would have surely been enough to validate Jesus in their eyes. But what happened next was extraordinary. The voice of the Father himself declared his approval from the heavens: *"This is my Son; I love him; listen to him."*

When God Almighty says listen, we must listen. Of all their astonishing experiences with Jesus, this one must have sealed the deal for the disciples. After this, how could they not follow him to the end?

- Do I understand that Jesus is more than my present understanding of him? What disciplines can I pursue in order to know him better?

- Moses and Elijah typify the law and the prophets. Is following Jesus greater than keeping the law to me? Is knowing Jesus greater than the power of God to me?

DIG DEEPER · *2 PETER 1:16–21; MATTHEW 3:13–17*

Father, you voiced your affirmation and
adoration of your Son on that mountaintop.
Help me to see Jesus in greater glory today than
I did yesterday. Help me to adore him as you do
and declare him to others today.

MIRACLES FROM THE HANDS OF MEN

DAY 10   *Luke 10:1–21*

"I saw Satan fall like lightning from heaven."

Jesus knew the ultimate demise of his Father's arch-enemy and was at work to bring it about. His prophetic destiny was to bruise the serpent's head, but here, in an unexpected turn, he extended the scope of this warfare.

"Behold, I have given you authority to tread on serpents and scorpions, and over all the power of the enemy." His own anointing to tread on the serpent was now to be fleshed out through his disciples. They were to work with him to reverse the curse. Imagine the sheer joy they must have known when they found they could do what he did.

Think of the fishermen who knew what it meant to toil and labor for a small catch. What did they feel when they saw their boats sinking with the weight of the catch? Think of Luke, who had dedicated his life to the noble trade of mending bodies with whatever meager medicine he had to work with. What thoughts flooded his head when he heard of Jesus instantly healing impossible cases—and when he traveled himself with an apostolic team who brought the same healing power to cities throughout Asia Minor?

They knew they could not do this in their own power. Yet there *was* a power working with them, soon to be in them, that ushered Heaven into the earth. Having touched such power, having shared such ministry with Jesus—what could they possibly do but follow him to the very end?

- What must the disciples have felt to have the very power of God working through them? Proud? Humbled? Confused?

- How might this experience have fueled and strengthened them to endure the hardships and martyrdom that was to come?

DIG DEEPER · *Acts 1:6–9; Luke 9:1–6*

Father, it is amazing to me that you would draft your followers into this spiritual warfare of your kingdom, that you would equip us for treading on serpents. Lord, I give you my hands and feet and voice. I am willing to be used in whatever way you would empower me today.

A FULL-ORBED MAN

DAY 11 | *LUKE 2:39–52*

At twelve years of age, Jesus got a taste of his ministry and declared that he must be about his Father's business. But he knew his times and seasons, and it was not yet time to go fully public. To do his Father's business at that moment meant to submit to his parents and grow.

Imagine…he had to grow.

Think of the Son of God *growing* in wisdom, stature, favor with God, and favor with man (mentally, physically, spiritually, socially). Imagine him tired in his body or weary in his mind. Consider him learning the scriptures and how to hear the voice of his Father. Think of him navigating the complex social customs of his day.

Jesus' disciples understood he was no mere man—he raised people from the dead and commanded the wind and waves. He transfigured before their very eyes, and God spoke to him aloud from the heavens. But he was also not some apparition. He was as human as any of them. He grew hungry, rejoiced with them, wept at the tomb of his friend, and suffered great anxiety before his death. He was a full-orbed man.

The disciples themselves were in the process of growing in all these areas. They were learning to submit to the working of the Holy Spirit and to live in love with one another.

They followed a rabbi who was fully human, but more than human. They knew a high priest who was able to sympathize with their weaknesses—who in every respect was tempted as they were, yet without sin.

- Has my understanding of Jesus been too much like a god of mythology? Do I see him as distant and unrelatable?

- Since Jesus experienced the fullness of life on Earth, can he be trusted to sympathize with me and help me in my areas of need?

DIG DEEPER · *Hebrews 4:14–16; 1 John 1:1–3*

Father, how good it is to have a Savior who knows what it is like to struggle mentally, physically, spiritually, and socially. How comforting to know that he can be trusted to help me in my day-to-day struggles. Teach me to run to him and receive the help I need.

SUPERNATURAL KNOWLEDGE

DAY 12   *MATTHEW 26:1–75*

Jesus knew the plot to kill him. He knew what was in Judas' heart and what the disciples were disputing among themselves. He knew what Peter would do in a few hours and that there was a man in the city who would lead them to the place where they would celebrate Passover. And he knew that the scriptures written about him would soon be fulfilled.

He predicted, with precise detail, events that would happen 40 years after his death. But more than knowing the future, he knew what was in the hearts of the men and women around him. Because of this, he did not put his trust in man, but in his Father.

Now when he was in Jerusalem at the Passover Feast, many believed in his name when they saw the signs that he was doing. But Jesus on his part did not entrust himself to them, because he knew all people and needed no one to bear witness about man, for he himself knew what was in man. (John 2:23–25)

This was not mere clairvoyance; in Jesus' case, it was omniscience. Being one with his Father meant that Jesus had all the knowledge of God. Yet, we never see him use that knowledge cynically, selfishly, or hurtfully (as humans would surely do). This knowledge caused his disciples to believe in him (John 16:30). Yet, surely what caught their imaginations was not just his omniscience, but his character—not merely his power, but how he held that power.

- If I were offered the gift of knowing all things, would I take it? What blessings might this bring into my life? What curses?

- Imagine the quality of character required to carry this type of knowledge without being greedy or self-seeking.

DIG DEEPER · *JOHN 2:23–25; PSALM 51*

*Lord Jesus, you know all things and you understand
the state of my heart. Grant that I may walk in honesty
and transparency before you and those around me today.
Purify my own motives day by day. Create in me a clean
heart and renew a right spirit within me.*

IRRESISTIBLE WISDOM

DAY 13   *MARK 12:1–44*

Jesus was the embodiment of wisdom. His hearers marveled at his words, for they were not like those of the sages, the Stoics, or even Solomon—no, they were much more than that. True wisdom is skill in the art of living. It hones strong character in a person. Even more, it reveals the heart of God.

Jesus spoke differently—and with perfect wisdom—to each of the different parties listed in this chapter. His answers depended on their hearts; and their responses laid their hearts bare for all to see.

- To the chief priests and teachers of the law, he told a simple story that plainly exposed their true intentions. They looked for a way to kill him.

- To the Pharisees and Herodians who ganged up on him to bring the scrutiny of Rome down upon him, he gave a simple answer that rendered them speechless: Give Caesar what is his, and give God what is his.

- To a poor widow, Jesus gave his affirmation and praise, lifting her up as an example (above the rich) because she gave all she had.

Sometimes the wisdom came in the form of questions designed to expose the heart: *Do you want to be whole? Was John's baptism from God or from man? Who do men say I am?*

Who do you say I am? Do you believe I am able to do this? Each question was perfectly tailored to the hearer and situation.

And he continued to answer them with such penetrating questions until "no one dared ask him any more questions." His wisdom shut the mouths of the wicked but opened the imaginations of the hungry.

- The Bible speaks of the wisdom of the world and the wisdom of God. What is the difference?

- The scriptures tell us that wisdom is more a person than a thing, that Christ is the power of God and the wisdom of God. How do I see the wisdom of God in the person of Jesus Christ?

DIG DEEPER · *James 3:13–18; 1 Corinthians 1:18–31*

*Father, I thank you that you have not left us in the dark,
but you have spoken your wisdom through your Son. I see
the foolishness of the world all around me, and I long to
walk in your wisdom. Please show me your ways, lead me
in your truth, and teach me by your Spirit.*

THERE IS ALWAYS MORE TO JESUS

DAY 14 | *LUKE 9:1–36*

They had heard him call them by name. This calling resonated so deeply in their souls that they left everything, rearranged their lives, and followed him. They heard him teach truth from another world with authority that could not be dismissed. They were with him as he performed miracles that had never been seen in Israel. They had even received authority from him to teach and heal in his name.

No wonder when Peter was asked who he thought Jesus was, his reply was, "the Messiah of God." They thought they knew him. But there is always more to know.

They had not yet seen him in his glory: his beyond-flesh-and-blood, bright-as-lightning, other-worldly glory. They did not yet understand that the two most revered men of their culture—the greatest law-giver and the greatest prophet—were merely preparers of the way for him; that he was the fulfillment of all their work.

There is always more of Jesus. All who heard of him held high opinions of who he was—but not high enough. A prophet? Someone great who had come back from the dead? Jesus was much more than that. Nicodemus knew he was a great teacher, a great miracle worker, someone who came from God. But he was much more. John experienced his entire earthly ministry, yet his vision on the Isle of Patmos went far beyond all he had seen previously. There is always more to Jesus.

- If I made a list of the things I know about Jesus, what would be on the list? What makes him unique among men?

- It is the job of the Spirit to reveal Jesus and enlighten his words to us. What can I do this week to receive greater revelation of who Jesus is?

DIG DEEPER · *REVELATION 1:9–20;*
COLOSSIANS 1:15–23

Father, what I have seen so far of Jesus has taken my breath away. I believe he is the most remarkable man who ever lived, yet I understand that I only know very little of him. Open my eyes to see him more and more each day. And help me to make him known to others.

LORD OF MY SEASONS

DAY 15   *MARK 5:21–43*

Two women, twelve years prior to this story. One woman pushes through the pain to give birth to a baby girl, the house ringing with joy and the hope of future generations. On the other side of town, a woman wakes to notice that something isn't right in her body. It is painful and persists, setting in motion a journey of fear and uncertainty, of sickness and despair, of spending everything on medical treatments that do no good.

Twelve years pass. Twelve years of living and loving, of pain and despondency. Both journeys come to a crossroads of desperation, and both stories intersect in one day in the life of Jesus.

He had crossed a violent sea and dealt with a demoniac. He had then made his way back across that same sea and down the streets of the town where these two women lived, each one drifting in her own personal storm. One carried a fleeting hope that her body shriveling from illness might be healed. The other wept beside a beautiful daughter of the Torah who teetered on the edge of death.

Jesus is Lord of our seasons. He is Lord of Time. He bursts onto the scene of our desperation and speaks the word that changes everything: *"Go in peace and be freed from your suffering." "Little girl, get up."* They may have been years in the making, but the emergencies were always on his schedule. And at the right time, everything comes together and the Sun of Righteousness rises with healing in his wings.

- What testimony do I have of Jesus showing up and meeting my need at just the right moment?
- What current fears in my life can be stilled by my remembering that Jesus Christ is Lord of Times?

DIG DEEPER · *PSALM 31:13–16; GALATIANS 4:1–5*

*Lord of all my seasons, lift me out of my limited
perspective and let me see things from your
vantage point. Grant me faith to know that my
times are firmly in your hands.*

PURGING THE THRESHING FLOOR

DAY 16   *LUKE 3:1–18*

The Baptizer came, burning with the Word of God, to the Jordan Valley—a valley with the lowest elevation on Earth—with his message to make way for the Lord. The call was clear: Repent and receive forgiveness of sins.

But how will God's salvation come? How will every valley be raised and every crooked way be made straight? Not by John, but by the one who comes after him. He will baptize not only with water, but with the Holy Spirit and with fire.

And there is more to the good news: He carries a winnowing fork in his hands to thoroughly purge his threshing floor. John refers to a process that was well known to his hearers: wheat threshing. The thresher would separate and gather the precious wheat but burn up the worthless chaff in the fire. He would perform this separation using whatever means necessary: the beating of rods, the trampling of an ox, a heavy threshing sledge. The skilled farmer would use the mildest means necessary to extract the grains from the stalks, but he would get the fruit out.

Luke says this process is part of the good news. Jesus will thoroughly purge his threshing floor. The Old Testament uses many metaphors for purifying God's people: the refiner's fire, the crucible, the fuller's soap, the wine press—

all for the purpose of separating and cleansing. This violent process is not meant to kill us, but to kill what is killing us, to set us free to be what God created us to be.

Extracting the precious from the worthless is part of the gospel. He will not only save us, but he will also sanctify us, make us his own, and bear fruit through us. Our job is to embrace the process.

- Imagine the kindness and holy zeal of the Father to rid me of things that hinder my holiness. He hates what hurts me and is active to purge those things from my life.

- Have I considered the sanctification process of the Holy Spirit a negative thing or an act of great love toward me?

DIG DEEPER · *Hebrews 12:1–11; Malachi 3:1–4*

*Father, I thank you for your heart to purge from me
the worthless things and cause the precious seed to grow
and bear fruit. The baptism of fire is a beautiful process.
Help me to recognize and welcome it and never to fight
your love when you express it in this way.*

JESUS VERSUS RELIGION

DAY 17 | *MATTHEW 23:1–36*

If we have lived long enough, we have learned that just because something is wrapped in a religious cloak doesn't mean it is holy. Pretend righteousness sets off our sham meter and we are repulsed by it.

Jesus attacked it with force. When his followers saw in him what authentic righteousness looks like, the veneer of those fakers stood in stark contrast.

Common people were drawn to Jesus because he modeled true spirituality and stood against the fakery. He unleashed his zeal against the religious system that did not represent his Father's true heart and purposes.

People living a false religion load others down with rules; they live life as a show before others; they love titles; they look beautiful on the outside but are full of rottenness.

While these religious leaders pronounced a woe upon the people, Jesus pronounced a woe upon them. He said the kingdom was to be taken from them and given to the tax collectors and the prostitutes.

For this reason, the religious leaders opposed him, but the common man heard him gladly. Jesus spoke up for the commands of God and against the traditions of men. Very few had the courage to do this because of the power those lying leaders held. But zeal for his Father's house consumed him. He desired mercy, not sacrifice (Matthew 9:13), and his followers loved him for it.

- In what ways has religious pride repulsed me? How is Jesus different from that kind of hubris?

- In what ways do I see religious pride in my life? How could following Jesus change that in me?

DIG DEEPER · *Mark 12:35–44; John 2:13–17*

Father, I see in your Son the beauty of real righteousness with no pretense or pride. Give me grace to see more and more of him and to do justice, love mercy, and walk humbly before you.

PRAYER

DAY 18   *JOHN 15:1–17*

His disciples saw it every day. It was the source of Jesus' life, the thing that made him different. The relationship he had with his Father was the fountain from which his entire life flowed.

His custom was to rise early and go to a quiet place to pray. He maintained a vital, constant relationship with Almighty God, calling on him in the most intimate of terms. And by taking his followers with him to that intimate place, he taught them to pray in the same way.

The models of prayer they had known to this point were hewn from rigid routine, a lifeless liturgy, stiff as stone. How could a common person rise to such an unattainable standard? But to Jesus, prayer was relationship, not ritual; love, not law; devotion, not duty.

For Jesus, prayer was not in the *doing* (getting everything right) but in the *being* (enjoying friendship with his Father). And out of that place of affection came his actions and power. The disciples saw him commune with his Father; they experienced the discourse between him and Heaven. They saw that he did nothing without first understanding the will and the ways of his Father.

This was the very thing they yearned for in their heart of hearts. As the deep of God called out to the deep in their own souls, they realized they were made for connection to their Maker. How could they taste of this and go back to what they had known?

- How has my culture taught me to pray? How is what I have learned from my culture different from the prayer life that Jesus modeled?

- Is there a mindset within me that needs to change so that real intimacy with the Father can be experienced?

DIG DEEPER · *John 16:23–27; Psalm 42:7–8*

Father, I see in Jesus the intimacy with you that I long for. Change my practice of prayer to look more like what I see in Jesus: more intimacy, less ritual. Let my abiding in you become the source of all my life.

BEAUTIFULLY, HUMBLY BOLD

DAY 19 | *Mark 11:1–33*

In the midst of Jesus' personal crucible, the disciples saw him display both raw emotion and perfect character. He never sought praise, but he did not deny it when it was given. He let the people worship him, for what they said was true. What they did fulfilled the scriptures.

Though he never deflected praise, he did not misuse his power. In fact, he judged those who abused their authority but were, like the fig tree, unfruitful. He did not appease the chief priests and teachers of the law. Rather, he laid the axe to the root of their hypocrisy.

He marched straight into the temple—the home of the most important thing God was doing on the earth at that time (communing with man and receiving man's worship)—and he overthrew that which misrepresented God, that which interrupted God's intimacy with man. He judged the greed that was wrapped in a cloak of worship.

Yet Luke, in his account, tells us that he wept over the city, longing for the people to know peace and mourning the destruction that was soon to come. His heart broke because they did not recognize the day when God visited them.

What kind of man can face fame with humility and mourn the very judgment he pronounces? What tables might he be overturning in us today? How might he be weeping over us?

- Imagine a man who can seethe over injustice and be moved to tears for those affected by it...and those who perpetrate it.
- Can I identify areas in my life that Jesus may want to overthrow and put right? Can I sense the empathy he feels for me?

DIG DEEPER · *LUKE 19:41–48; ROMANS 2:1–11*

*Father, I thank you for the bold and humble
Jesus, who hates the things that destroy me and
yet pours his compassion on me. Today, I yield to
his conviction and his comfort.*

WALKING THE EXTRA MILE

DAY 20   *Mark 16:1–11*

Jesus, with great compassion, walks the extra mile for those who are faithful, yet fearful.

Put yourself in Peter's shoes. Feel the failure and self-hate that must have eaten away at him after his denial of Jesus and the consuming sense of dread on those dark days following the crucifixion.

When Jesus sent this messenger to the tomb, he could have easily had him say, "Go, tell his disciples..." That would have sufficed. But the beautiful heart of Jesus wanted Peter to be restored, not sifted. He sent Peter a special, singled-out message: "But go, tell his disciples and Peter..." Jesus wanted Peter to know he was thinking especially of him.

Mary, who had been hopelessly possessed by demons and then redeemed and restored by the Master, came to anoint his body after his death. She had traveled with him from Galilee to Jerusalem. She stood with him at the cross. Now, she was the first one at the tomb.

She had been faithful, but now she was fearful and full of questions. She heard the truth heralded by the messenger at the tomb, and she was commissioned as the first evangelist. But she fled with the other women, trembling and bewildered. She did not tell anyone the good news at the word of the angel.

But, even in her fear and uncertainty, Jesus appeared to her and called her name (John 20:16). What a beautiful Savior who calls us by name! And his words changed everything—she was filled with boldness and went to tell everyone the good news.

Isaiah said of the Messiah, "a bruised reed he will not break, and a faintly burning wick he will not quench." Jesus, with great empathy and kindness, goes above and beyond to steady his faithful, fearful followers.

- How has the Savior come to me in gentleness and assurance amid my seasons of doubt and fear?

- Is there a time when I heard the Master call me by name? Have I heard a personalized word that gave me strength and lifted me out of fear?

DIG DEEPER · *JOHN 20:1–18; ISAIAH 42:1–7*

*Father, what tenderness and care you show to me
when I am doubting you and myself. How beautiful
to hear you say my name when circumstances seem
to hide your face. Help me to see and receive your
kindness during my times of fear.*

A SECURE LEADER

DAY 21 | *LUKE 10:1–20*

Insecure men with power are the scourge of history. They centralize control around themselves and work hard to keep it from others. They plot and scheme and push their plans… and many people suffer because of them.

But Jesus is different. Although he possessed power and authority that despots only dream of, he didn't keep it to himself. He was so secure that he gave it away to his students. In the previous chapters, he called, taught, trained, sent, retrained, and now resends them. He released and decentralized his power.

This is the way of things with the Trinity. The Father gives the Son; the Son gives his power away; the Spirit gives gifts to men and women to enable them for the task. Not only to his inner circle, but also to 72 others, Jesus said, "I trust you with my harvest…I empower you to preach and heal… If they reject you, they reject me and the one who sent me."

"I saw Satan fall like lightning." Dripping with pride, centralizing power, gathering for himself the worship he was meant to pass along to God—this was the fall of Lucifer. "I will be like the Most High." (Isaiah 14:14)

But Jesus says, "I will empty myself." Who wouldn't follow and give all for this man? He freely gives to his followers the things that prophets and angels long for. He is the most secure leader history has ever known.

- Imagine a man with ultimate power who is bent on using it for good. Imagine him giving this power away to others.

- What kind of good could a person accomplish on this earth if there was no concern for who got the credit? How does God want to give his authity to me? Who might I bless today with his power?

DIG DEEPER · *MATTHEW 28:16–20; COLOSSIANS 1:15–23*

Father, history tells the tale of so many who have wreaked havoc because they held their power with closed fists and insecure souls. Grant me the freedom to be able to see your kingdom expand without having to receive credit myself.

DEEP DIVISIONS

The opinions about Jesus could not have been more extreme. Some said he was a good man, others that he was a deceiver. Some claimed he was the Messiah, others that he was demon-possessed.

It is impossible to hold both opinions. We must decide, and the side we come down on depends on what we love.

Toward the end of Jesus' ministry, tension was building. His life and his teaching caused deep divisions among the people. The written Word of God divides soul and spirit; the Living Word divides perhaps even deeper. The decision became clearer: They were either for him or against him.

Here we see so many wrong ideas about the Messiah. Where does he come from? A place? A lineage? But what Jesus clearly said took the divisions to the deepest level: *You know where I am from; I am from God. I am the one this feast speaks of—I am living water.*

Then he drove the wedge even deeper and made the chasm uncrossable: *I am from above; you are from below. I am not of this world; you are of this world. I am of my Father in heaven; you are of your father, the devil, for you are liars and murderers like he is.*

I AM. This was the final straw. He took on the most holy name of God. He claimed deity. This man had to be stopped.

- What kind of divisions do the words of Jesus bring to my soul?

- What difference does my belief in him make in the way I live my life today?

DIG DEEPER · *MATTHEW 10:32–39; LUKE 12:49–53*

Father, I believe Jesus is the Son of God. I pray
for strength and courage to stand for that belief.
I pray that this belief may guide my actions
toward others today.

BRUISING THE SERPENT'S HEAD

DAY 23　　　*JOHN 12:17–36*

The very first prophecy of the coming Messiah, uttered immediately after the fall in the garden of Eden, told of the epic battle between the serpent and the offspring of Eve. God himself pronounced this judgment upon the serpent:

"And I will put enmity between you and the woman, and between your offspring and her offspring; he shall bruise your head, and you shall bruise his heel." (Genesis 3:15)

Everywhere Jesus went, his disciples witnessed his foot come down on the head of the serpent. He brought health where there was sickness, life where there was death, justice where injustice had reigned. He spoke truth that brought freedom to those bound by lies. He put right the wrong ideas about God among his people.

And he would do all of this, not by might nor power, but by the Spirit of the Lord. He would bring it about through his death on the cross, and he would draw all people to himself.

The thief comes to steal, kill, and destroy; Jesus comes with gifts and life and restoration. Before their very eyes they saw the perfect fulfillment of God's prophetic plan to restore the earth and mankind.

Jesus put it this way: The ruler of this world is cast out. (12:31) John, who witnessed the entirety of Jesus' serpent-crushing work, would later write, "*The reason the Son of God appeared was to destroy the works of the devil.*" (1 John 3:8)

They saw a world oppressed by sin and sickness being transformed before their eyes. Who would not follow this man? Who would not give all for this kingdom?

- Imagine the adrenaline that must have flowed through the disciples as they saw the word of the prophets come to pass before their eyes. What must it have been like to see things set right by the word and power of Jesus?

- Are there works of the enemy around me that need crushing? How might God use me through prayer and actions to see the power of Jesus prevail there?

DIG DEEPER · *Hebrews 2:5–18; Revelation 20:1–15*

Father, I marvel at the prophecy-fulfilling, justice-bringing, head-crushing power of your Son, Jesus. Thank you for the fulfillment of this promise, and may the power of Jesus work through me to bruise the serpent's head.

A LIFE BEYOND MYSELF

DAY 24   *JOHN 12:1–50*

The disciples followed Jesus, willing to give all for their Lord, because he gave them a greater vision for their lives than merely existing. When God created us in his own image, he set eternity in our hearts. We are made for eternal things; living for our own comfort and protecting our own reputation is far below our purpose.

The quicker we understand this, the better we will live our lives. And the Lord of Life taught his disciples that the key to living is dying.

"The hour has come for the Son of Man to be glorified." But how? By falling to the earth and dying in order to produce life in others. This is the very reason he came into the world, and this is the way God would receive glory through him.

The opportunity to lose our lives is what Jesus offers us. The paradox is this: When we lose our life, we find it. When we die, we live. When we say no to our own way, we find the best way. This is the upside-down kingdom of God.

Humanity seems doomed to look for purpose in the smallest and vainest of places. But there is glory in giving all for God and for others. Jesus' disciples caught that vision and decided to live and die for him. Church tradition says that these men went to Greece, Turkey, Ukraine, Ethiopia, India, Arabia, North Africa, Syria, Italy, and Persia—all of them dying for the One who gave his life for all. We are the fruit of their lives.

- What experiences have I had where giving up my rights has caused me to live a richer, fuller life?
- What might God be calling me to give up in order to bring glory to his name?

DIG DEEPER · *PHILIPPIANS 1:19–21; ECCLESIASTES 3:9–11*

Father, I have tasted the emptiness of this world. I know that it does not deliver on its promises, and it cannot satisfy me. I believe that I will truly find my life when I lay it down for you. Give me vision and courage to die to self and live for you.

REMEMBERING

<table>
<tr><td>DAY 25</td><td>LUKE 22:1–71</td></tr>
</table>

Memory can be a fuel that strengthens our resolve. By looking back, we can receive fresh bearings for moving forward. We read these gospel passages in retrospect. They were, of course, written in retrospect as the disciples remembered that night. It was in constantly revisiting these memories that their courage to follow Jesus was strengthened.

They remembered how the Passover, which they had celebrated from their youth, took on a whole new meaning: The Lamb is a person; *his* body broken, *his* blood poured out for them.

They recalled the sting of the rebuke as they argued over who was greatest. And Jesus' example of a leader: fully focused on the mission, willing to serve, surrendering to darkness for love's sake.

They relived Peter's denial, Judas' kiss, and Jesus' prayer to the Father: "Not my will, but yours."

Remembering was an important part of the Jewish culture the disciples grew up in. All their lives they had sung Psalms that recounted the awesome works of God for their ancestors. They took part in yearly feasts and festivals that recalled God's faithfulness as he intervened for them in times of difficulty (Passover, Booths, Purim).

The purpose of these feasts was to remind them of God's covenant love even in the face of their own struggles.

Remembering kept the disciples' perspective true and strengthened them for the sacrifices they would have to make for the sake of Christ.

- How have I been strengthened by remembering my experiences with Jesus?
- Are those memories building courage for new exploits to which God may be calling me?

DIG DEEPER · *Psalm 136; Ephesians 2:11–13*

Father, I see your hand moving in mercy throughout my life. Let me never forget your kindness to me. Strengthen my resolve to serve you as I remember your faithfulness to me.

EXAMINED & FOUND TO BE SPOTLESS

DAY 26   *LUKE 23:1–49*

Few things convinced Jesus' followers of his deity (and his humanity) as did his crucifixion. Though they did not understand when Jesus told them it would happen, the prophetic scriptures concerning the Messiah were played out before them in graphic detail.

They saw him submit to a mock trial, to beating, and to a horrible death as a punishment for sins he never committed. Arch rivals became close friends because of their common hatred of him. His disciples were ready to fight for him, but Jesus told them to put down their swords (Luke 22:49–51). This king's reign would come about in a different way.

They watched supernatural things happen at his death. The sun failed to shine at midday, an earthquake opened the graves of many saints, and the veil in the Jewish temple that forbade entrance into the holiest place was ripped in two, starting at the top—as if God himself did the tearing. Even the Roman soldier standing by the cross recognized that Jesus must have been the Son of God.

There was no crime here. Like thousands of lambs that Passover night, Jesus was examined and found to be spotless, worthy of being sacrificed for the sins of the people.

There were a few on his side: Simon, the African who helped to bear his cross; the women who were with him at a distance; Joseph, who asked for his body and put him in a proper resting place. They saw his innocence and felt the pathos of his sacrifice. They saw his true worth and committed to follow him, no matter the cost.

- How did such a scene of holiness, devastation, and death solidify the disciples' resolve to follow Jesus?

- How does Christ's innocence change the meaning of the crucifixion?

DIG DEEPER · *Isaiah 53:1–12; John 12:23–26*

Father, the innocence and obedience of your Son has captured me. Seeing his unreserved sacrifice makes me want to lose my life for his sake. Help me to give way to your will as Jesus did that I might bear fruit for you today.

THE PSALMS SHOUT

DAY 27   *JOHN 19:1–42*

The religious leaders had chosen their sides. The Father arranged those in power as pawns to bring about his purpose. They locked arms with their Roman enemies to sentence Jesus to death. They demanded an insurrectionist—one who had plotted against Rome—be released instead of Jesus. They lied boldly: "We have no king but Caesar!"

Now the most convincing sign that Jesus was the Messiah was played out in front of them in real time—a real-life depiction of Psalm 22. When Jesus quoted the opening lines of the Psalm, he was signaling, for all who could hear it, his own fulfillment of the Messianic poem.

- Psalm 22:1—"My God, my God, why have you forsaken me?"
- Psalm 22:7—"All who see me mock me"
- Psalm 22:8—"He trusts in the Lord; let him deliver him"
- Psalm 22:15—"my strength is dried up like a potsherd, and my tongue sticks to my jaws"
- Psalm 22:16—"a company of evildoers encircles me"
- Psalm 22:16—"they have pierced my hands and feet"
- Psalm 22:18—"they divide my garments among them, and for my clothing they cast lots."
- Psalm 22:31—"he has done it." (It is finished)

It is as if David were present at the cross and wrote those words after the event. This is extraordinary since this method of punishment was not widely used until hundreds of years after David penned the words. For anyone with ears to hear and eyes to see, it would have been obvious that Jesus was the Messiah—the one who fulfilled Psalm 22 so we could live in the reality of Psalm 23.

- What are the odds that David predicted, in the poetic description of the events of his own life, the graphic detail of the scene at the cross?

- God's plan of redemption, conceived from the foundation of the world, was foretold in many ways through prophets and poets. Does this strengthen my own faith?

DIG DEEPER · *PSALM 22–23; ACTS 2:14–36*

Father, you gave a perfect picture of the suffering of your Son thousands of years before it happened—the depiction is stunning and clear. I believe Jesus is the Messiah who was foretold. Give me boldness to share this truth with those around me who are desperate for a Savior.

RESURRECTION

DAY 28   *LUKE 24:1–12*

If the manner of his death was life-changing to Jesus' followers, how much more was seeing him alive again? Why did they commit their lives to this man without reservation? The simple answer is this: They saw him die, they saw him buried, and they saw him alive again.

He rose from the dead—just as he said he would do—they spoke with him for forty days, and then he was carried into Heaven before their eyes.

The resurrection of Jesus was the constant message of the early church. It validated all that Jesus Christ said about himself. It assures me that I can be forgiven and have the power to live a brand new life. It means that Jesus Christ is present and active in my life today, and it ensures that I will be resurrected also.

In the sermons of Jesus' apostles, the cross is never viewed apart from the resurrection. This is what elevates Christianity above the world of religious ideas and sets it in the realm of life-changing relationship with the living God. The resurrection is not just a historical event (though it is that), but an event that breaks into history now, with the power of another world.

If Jesus Christ has not risen from the dead, his promises are proven false. The resurrection was God's stamp of approval on the person, message, and sacrifice of his Son. We are not asked to merely believe the doctrine of the resurrection. We are called upon to meet this person who was raised from the dead.

- The message of the apostles was, *"We have seen him. He is alive! Now you must respond."* Why does the message of the resurrection always demand a response from the hearer?

- What difference should the extraordinary message of Christ's resurrection make in my life?

DIG DEEPER · *1 CORINTHIANS 15:1–8; ROMANS 6:1–14*

Father, you have opened my eyes to the truth that your Son is alive forever. Let my life reflect his resurrection power. Help me understand that as you have raised Christ from the dead, you have raised me to newness of life. Give me grace and courage to pass this life on to others.

SLOW HEARTS, BURNING HEARTS

DAY 29   *LUKE 24:13–53*

Was Jesus being playful? Why did he interact with his followers in this way at such an important moment? It almost seems like he was playing hide-and-seek with them. At the very least, he surprised them in peculiar ways.

They thought him to be in the tomb, but he walked, unrecognized, with two men along the road. He played ignorant to the events at Jerusalem. He opened the scriptures to them, showing them things they never saw before about him. He broke bread and then disappeared from their sight. He appeared out of nowhere to his disciples and asked for food to eat. He opened the scriptures to them too. He said the Father had a gift for them but while he was blessing them, he rose into Heaven and disappeared.

Why would he do it like that? Perhaps we can think of more dignified ways for one to show himself alive from the grave. But Jesus knows how to reveal himself to us and change us in the most lasting ways.

How wonderful and beautiful and playful and wise is Jesus. How life-giving are his words. Above all, he turned their slow hearts into burning hearts by a fresh revelation of himself and a fresh reading of the scriptures—the scriptures that reveal and point to him. He will do the same for us every day if we let him.

- How has Jesus shown himself to me in unexpected ways?
- Can I remember a time when a fresh revelation of Jesus turned my "slow heart" into a "burning heart"?

DIG DEEPER · *1 John 1:1–3; Ephesians 1:15–23*

Father, I understand that left to myself, my heart can become calloused and discouraged. I need a fresh revelation of your Son and your scriptures to help me live in the everyday expectancy of your kingdom coming around me. Fill me to overflowing so I can pour out to others.

FOLLOW ME

DAY 30   *JOHN 21:1–25*

We don't know why Peter and the others went back to fishing. Perhaps in an uncertain time, the certainty of doing what was familiar brought comfort. Maybe it was the one thing in their lives they felt they had control over. Maybe they were just laying low, hoping the officials would not come for them. Or they simply needed money to feed their families.

But Jesus came to them to communicate that things were not winding down, but rather just gearing up. And he did it in a most effective way, repeating a miracle they had experienced at the start. When he filled their nets with fish again, they remembered the wonder they felt when they were first called to follow him.

They felt the assurance that his original call on their lives to be fishers of men was not finished. Peter would soon cast a net to a group of Jewish pilgrims and later to a God-fearing Gentile and his household—and the world would never be the same.

Do you love me? Feed my sheep! Remember what I have made you to be and don't shrink back. Do not count your life as precious to you. Whatever it takes, this is your calling until you die for me, as I have died for you: "Follow me."

Will we do the same? Will we refuse the temptation to compare ourselves with others? Jesus says, "Leave those thoughts alone and follow me." Can you hear the same call that these men heard? Will you dare to leave all to follow this extraordinary man?

- Do I find Jesus Christ worth surrendering all for?
- Do I hear a specific call to do something daring for Christ? Have I shrunk back from that call? Is it time to renew my purpose to follow him?

DIG DEEPER · *Mark 1:16–20; Acts 10:1–48*

Father, I can hear you calling out to me to venture from my safe shore and follow you into the deep waters. It is my desire to give my life for you as you gave your life for me. Take me, guide me, empower me to follow you all the way to the end.

INTRODUCTION

BOOK THREE

The Holy Spirit is the very presence of Almighty God, gifted to us by a loving Father and a generous Son. He is the promise and power of God, active every day in the lives of Christ-followers.

The Bible teaches that the Holy Spirit is a person and is one part of the Trinity, eternally existent with the Father and the Son and equally important. Every Christ-follower should be educated, equipped, and expectant regarding the work of the Holy Spirit in their lives and within the body of Christ.

So what does the Bible say about God, the Holy Spirit? This devotional is a survey of the early church—followers of Jesus who were learning how to walk in this new gift of the Spirit. Through their stories we discover the many ways the Holy Spirit works in us to reveal and glorify Jesus Christ and to draw us to God the Father.

DAILY READINGS

Day 1 — The Promise of Presence — *Acts 1:1–5*

Day 2 — Every Day Is "With Day" — *John 14:15–18*

Day 3 — Making Much of the Father & the Son — *Acts 7:48–56*

Day 4 — Mystery & Wonder — *2 Corinthians 13:11–14*

Day 5 — Filled with the Spirit — *John 14:16–17*

Day 6 — Attributes of a Person — *1 Corinthians 2:10–16*

Day 7 — The Holy Spirit Reveals Jesus — *John 16:12–14*

Day 8 — Woven into God's Tapestry — *Acts 4:23–31*

Day 9 — Power to Witness — *Acts 2:37–41*

Day 10 — Plunged into Community — *Acts 4:32–35*

Day 11 — Shining Light on Scripture — *Acts 2:14–21*

Day 12 — Plunged into Prayer — *Acts 2:41–42*

Day 13 — The Hour of Prayer — *Acts 3:1–10*

Day 14 — How Do I Pray? — *Romans 8:26–27*

Day 15 — Made Holy by the Spirit — *Acts 5:1–11*

Day 16 — Through Every Believer — *Acts 6:1–7*

Day 17 — Keeping in Step with the Spirit — *Acts 10:1–33*

Day 18 — The Spirit Helps Our Marriages — *Ephesians 5:18–33*

Day 19 — Meeting the Needs of the Body — *Romans 12:3–8*

Day 20 — New Birth — *Acts 2:37–39*

Day 21 — Bears Fruit in Us — *Galatians 5:22–25*

Day 22 — The Spirit Speaks to Us — *Acts 8:26–40*

Day 23 — Our Guide into Truth — *John 16:12–15*

THE PROMISE OF PRESENCE

DAY 1   *ACTS 1:1–5*

Don't go anywhere until you receive the promise of the Father.

For three-and-a-half years Jesus' disciples walked with him. They saw how he lived, how he listened to the Father and spoke what he heard. His teaching revolutionized them. They saw the religious and political leaders turn against him. They saw him die and lay in a tomb for days. But now—just imagine—they see him alive again, and they walk and talk with him!

Surely he would now reign as king of his own kingdom on the earth. But Jesus had a different kind of kingdom in mind. And what was coming would require a power they knew nothing of as yet. Jesus had told them about a promise the Father had made—a gift to them of his presence and his power. This was a further fulfillment of the promise made to Moses thousands of years ago.

Moses was preparing to leave Sinai with God's chosen people (Exodus 33). After centuries of waiting, this was the privileged generation that would finally see the promised land. But their stubborn contempt for Yahweh had changed everything. God would drive out the inhabitants; he would usher his people into the promised land—but he would not go there with them.

Moses' response turned God's heart: *The promise is nothing without the presence.*

And this is the wisdom for us: The presence of God is more to be desired than the promises of God. Of all the great things God has in store for us, none of them is more valuable than our relationship with him. For as Moses rightly said, this is what makes God's people different from all other people: He goes with us.

- Has my spiritual life been characterized by looking for the promise of God or the presence of God?

- How does God's presence make a difference in my day-to-day life? My family? My community?

DIG DEEPER · *Exodus 33:1–4,12–17; John 14:15–16*

Father, how incredible it is that you have made a covenant promise to be with me. Truly, your presence with me is more of a treasure than your promises to me. May your presence change me and work through me today for your glory.

EVERY DAY IS "WITH DAY"

DAY 2   *JOHN 14:15–18*

The normally busy streets of the port city I was visiting were empty and quiet. Since this was a tourist city I was puzzled, so I asked my guide where everyone was.

"Oh, it's a holiday today," he replied.

Confused, I responded, "I didn't realize that. Which holiday?"

"Today is *With Day*."

"Excuse me, I'm not familiar with that day."

"Oh, you call it Pentecost—it's the day the Holy Spirit came to be with us."

That response exploded in my soul. This annual holiday celebrates a historical event, but for believers, every day of our lives is *With Day*!

Jesus, in his generosity, asked the Father to give us a gift, and the generous Father responded by sending us a Helper. What an extraordinary gift this Helper is to us. He is sent to our side to assist us, whatever the need.

The Spirit stands for us, pleading our cause before the Father. He teaches us the culture and customs of this new kingdom we have been brought into. He is the means by which God grants us help from his throne of grace in our time of need.

The words that Scripture uses to describe the work of the Spirit are personal words. "You know him, for he dwells with you and will be in you." (John 14:17b)

Jesus said the personal, daily aid of this Helper will be the normal experience for every believer. And his help is not temporary; he will be with us forever. Not a single day of our lives are we without help from above. Every day is With Day.

- How conscious am I of the moment-to-moment presence of the Spirit each day?

- In what ways can I become more aware of and responsive to the Spirit's help?

DIG DEEPER · *Romans 8:26–27; Exodus 33:12–17*

Father, how needy I am and how generous you are to give your Spirit to be my Helper every day. Remind me of this help and make my heart sensitive to your instruction, your leading, and your conviction.

MAKING MUCH OF THE FATHER & THE SON

DAY 3   *ACTS 7:48–56*

As one God, eternally existing in three persons, the members of the Trinity live in perfect community. They do not struggle for power within their relationship or exalt themselves above the others. They submit and defer to one another, not because they have no choice, but because they have one mind.

In creation, in redemption, and in mission, they are in agreement, and each fulfills his role to accomplish these purposes. But the Spirit has a particular focus on glorifying the Father and the Son.

The Holy Spirit always leads men to glorify God. He searches, knows, and reveals the God of glory. *"For the Spirit searches everything, even the depths of God. For who knows a person's thoughts except the spirit of that person, which is in him? So also no one comprehends the thoughts of God except the Spirit of God."* (1 Corinthians 2:10–11)

As Jesus had come to reveal and so glorify the Father, so the Holy Spirit came to reveal and so glorify the Son (John 16:14). Jesus sent the Spirit to his followers so they could continue to know him, and the Spirit carries on Jesus' mission of revealing the Father.

Filled with the Spirit, Stephen spoke of the eternal dominion of the Father and saw the glory of the Son. The heart, mind, and purposes of the Eternal God are revealed to us through the work of the Holy Spirit.

- In what ways have I experienced the Holy Spirit revealing the Father to me?

- How has the Spirit opened my eyes to see Jesus more clearly?

DIG DEEPER · *1 Corinthians 2:9–11; John 15:26*

Father, I am grateful for the gift of the Spirit who opens my mind to understand your heart and the heart of your Son. I open my heart to you, that you may reveal the depths of who you are and what you want in ever-increasing measure.

MYSTERY & WONDER

DAY 4 | *2 CORINTHIANS 13:11–14*

Belief in God is a commitment to mystery because it is not possible for finite humans to fully comprehend the infinite God. Almighty God reveals himself to us as one being, eternally existent in three persons. The Father is God, the Son is God, the Spirit is God—yet there is one God. It is an unfathomable mystery, a truth we take by faith.

What did Paul mean when he wrote to young believers and spoke of the *fellowship of the Holy Spirit*? The Holy Spirit possesses all the attributes of God: He is holy, eternal, all-knowing, all-powerful, all-present. He is not a created being; he has always existed and is fully God.

And now, through faith in Christ, our hearts once dead in sin have been made alive, and that very Spirit lives in us. This, too, is a mystery we must take by faith. This is the stunning truth that Paul lays before the believers in Corinth: God himself has come to take up residence within them. Their spirits were made new by the very Spirit of the Living God.

The direct result of John 3:16 is 1 Corinthians 3:16: We are God's temple. God's Spirit lives not only among the gathered body of believers, but also within individual believers (1 Corinthians 6:19–20). This indwelling changes everything, and it ushers wonder into our daily lives.

- Do the mysteries of God deter me or intrigue me?
- How do the Father, Son, and Spirit work together to bring about the purposes of God?

DIG DEEPER · *1 Corinthians 2:9–11; 6:19–20*

Father, the mystery of your three-in-oneness
challenges my mind but excites my spirit. I thank you
for the wonder of your presence living in me. Your
Spirit with me is a gift beyond measure.

FILLED WITH THE SPIRIT

DAY 5   *JOHN 14:16–17*

Jesus said the unthinkable to his disciples: The Spirit is *with* you now, but he will be *in* you. The active work of the Holy Spirit in the life of the believer is not an option; it is crucial. It is the normal Christian experience.

If you have had a powerful experience of the Holy Spirit, that was not the end; that was the entrance into a life. We should be thankful for every experience, but we should not look to any one experience as "the" experience. The Spirit-filled life should be an ongoing, lifelong experience of empowerment and change, led by the wonderful, ever-present Holy Spirit.

A good example is Stephen, a powerful witness to Jesus in the early church who was one filled with the Holy Spirit (Acts 6:5). This didn't refer to an experience, but to a lifestyle of having the fruit and gifts of the Spirit operating in his life. And it was evident to all around him.

Jesus said it was necessary for him to go away so that he could send the Helper to be with us and in us. We should never be content to say, "I believe in Christ, and that is enough." God redeemed us to himself so that we could have a living, vibrant relationship with him through the Holy Spirit.

- Have I seriously considered the importance of being filled with the Holy Spirit?
- Have I thought the filling of the Spirit to be an experience or a lifestyle?

DIG DEEPER · *JOHN 16:7–11; EPHESIANS 5:18*

Father, thank you that the indwelling Holy Spirit is constantly deepening my relationship with you and empowering my witness for Christ. Through this power, may I make a difference in my world today.

ATTRIBUTES OF A PERSON

DAY 6   *1 CORINTHIANS 2:10–16*

Two errors threaten to stunt our spiritual growth. The first is to think of God as too distant and unreachable; the second, that God is too human-like and familiar. The scriptures teach us that God is both beyond us and near to us, unknowable and relational. The error comes when we are out of balance on one side or the other.

The Bible is clear that the Holy Spirit is divine, but that he also has the attributes of a person. He is not an impersonal thing, but a personal being; a "he", not an "it". The Spirit speaks (Acts 1:16) and has a mind (1 Corinthians 2:10–11), emotions (Ephesians 4:30), and a will (1 Corinthians 12:11). Like you and me, he can be lied to (Acts 5:3) and resisted (Acts 7:51).

Paul tells the young believers that the Spirit works within them to help them know what is in God's mind and what is in their own minds. Perhaps it is difficult to think of a spirit as having human qualities. Yet, the Holy Spirit works together with our humanness.

When we walk by the Spirit, his love and peace are reflected through us. In our emotions we can feel his empathy or anger. There is a holy synergy between the Spirit's personal attributes and our own humanity. This makes co-working with the Spirit possible.

- Do I tend to see God as too distant or too familiar? How might he want to challenge me to be more balanced in my thinking?
- How can the Holy Spirit work through my human thoughts? My emotions? My will?

DIG DEEPER · *Isaiah 11:1–4; Acts 5:1–11*

*Father, I thank you for the gift of the Holy Spirit.
I am grateful for the holy alliance between your
Spirit and my humanness. Help me to listen better
and respond to his moving.*

THE HOLY SPIRIT REVEALS JESUS

DAY 7 *JOHN 16:12–14*

There is always more of Jesus to know. We are unable to comprehend the depths of Christ without help, but God has given us this help through his Spirit. Any truth we come to know about the Son of God, we come to know only through the revelation of the Spirit.

Jesus tells his disciples that he has a lot more to say to them, but the time is not right. Then he tells them how the Spirit will work in their lives. He will not speak whatever he wants, but he will speak what he hears from the Father (just like Jesus). He will also show them things that are to come.

Our walk with God is a journey of growing in the knowledge of this One who is the image of the invisible God. The particular assignment of the Spirit is to take the things of Jesus—who he is, what he has done—and declare them to us.

The Spirit reveals the work of Jesus, applies that work to our lives, and works to conform us into his image. He unleashes the power of the words of Christ. He makes his greatness greater, his sweetness sweeter, and his grace more gracious and amazing to us. The more the Spirit is at work in our lives, the more in awe of Jesus we will be.

- How aware am I of my need for the Spirit's intervention in my growth in Christ?

- How has the Holy Spirit shown me deeper insights about the work of Jesus?

DIG DEEPER · *John 14:25–26; 1 John 2:27*

Father, reveal the Son of God to me in ever-increasing measure. May your Spirit open my eyes to the treasures of Christ and empower me to make him known to those around me.

WOVEN INTO GOD'S TAPESTRY

DAY 8   *ACTS 4:23–31*

The Kingdom of God is about change. The blind see, the lame walk, the dead live again, and the good news is preached to the poor. Wherever the reign of God breaks into a place, it brings the culture of the Kingdom—the culture of Heaven—to that place.

Here the first believers, made alive and emboldened by the Spirit inside them, got to see the bigger picture of God's purpose. The scriptures came alive to them as they understood that David's words in Psalm 2 applied to their own struggles. They saw themselves in the tapestry of God's big-picture redemptive plan.

A threshold has been crossed in the dealings between God and man. Now the very presence of God is living and active among us at all times. When we see ourselves as a thread in God's tapestry, everything changes for us. We endure hardship because there is eternal purpose in it. Filled with the Spirit, we open our mouths as ambassadors of this new kingdom. We break out of the fear and apathy and we embrace newness.

Perhaps the discontentment we often feel is because God has primed us for change—and for fulfilling our place in his eternal plan.

- What threshold may I be standing at today? What new place is God beckoning me to?

- Do I feel stuck in the status quo? Do I expect the Holy Spirit to expand my vision and give me boldness to enter new places?

DIG DEEPER · *ACTS 2:14–21; PSALM 2:1–8*

Father, I am amazed to be part of your family and your eternal plan. I see that you have made me on purpose for your purpose in this time. Give me eyes to see the new places you are challenging me to and give me courage to step across the threshold.

POWER TO WITNESS

DAY 9 | *Acts 2:37–41*

The disciples began to experience something they had never known before. They found themselves becoming natural witnesses to what God had done for them. And the source of their power was not themselves. Through his Spirit, our God gives us power to naturally (and supernaturally) bear witness of Christ and be an active part in the mission of his kingdom.

In a courtroom, a witness merely describes what he or she has seen and knows to be true. The same is true with witnessing for God. He wants to fill us up so that we can effectively offer the hope we have found in Jesus to others. God invites us into the mission of his kingdom.

Jesus told his disciples to go into all the world and preach the gospel. He told them that signs would follow those who believe. And we are told that "they went out and preached everywhere, while the Lord worked with them and confirmed the message by accompanying signs." (Mark 16:20)

If we ask the Father for a "mission mindset", if we open our eyes and ears to those God has put around us, if we rehearse our story and are willing to tell it, then we can expect the Holy Spirit to make us natural witnesses for Christ. It is our responsibility to go and speak the gospel. It is his promise to follow our going with signs and wonders.

- How might the adventure level in my life rise if I asked for a "mission mindset"?
- Who around me needs to hear a story of hope in Jesus?

DIG DEEPER · *ACTS 1:4–8; 8:4–8*

Father, I thank you that your Spirit inside me is the source of power for witness. Would you allow me to hear your invitation to be a partner in your mission? Would you open doors for me to tell my story today?

PLUNGED INTO COMMUNITY

DAY 10 | *ACTS 4:32–35*

Perhaps the first act of the Holy Spirit in our regenerated lives is to baptize us into the community of believers (1 Corinthians 12:12–13). As we grow in Jesus, we can expect the Holy Spirit to join us deeper in fellowship with other believers.

The first church was united in this community—together in the temple, together in their homes, sharing their possessions, looking for those who were in need and meeting those needs. All were of one heart and mind. This is the culture of the Kingdom.

Imagine a group whose members' passion and will were one. The work of the Spirit killed greed and selfishness. Because their very hearts were changed, they shared extraordinary community in the most ordinary of activities: They broke bread together.

There is something special about breaking bread. Perhaps this is why covenants were made around meals. Two necessities of life are met at once as our bodies and our souls are nourished by shared bounty. Fellowship and sustenance, knowledge of one another, the appreciation of differences— and the realization that in this body every joint supplies the needs of others.

- How have I experienced nourishment in the community of believers?

- How do I see God meeting my needs through others? How might he use me to meet their needs?

DIG DEEPER · *Ephesians 4:1–7, 15–16*

Father, I thank you for immersing me in this big, beautiful, diverse body of Christ. Help me to humbly receive what my brothers and sisters have and to freely give them what I can offer. Help me understand how I need those around me and how I can serve them.

SHINING LIGHT ON SCRIPTURE

DAY 11   *ACTS 2:14–21*

For more than three years the disciples heard Jesus explain his works and ways through interpreting the Old Testament scriptures. His ministry brought the scriptures to life, and the disciples now understood better the words they had heard as children.

Now Jesus was gone, but the descended Spirit would continue the work of shining divine light on the Word of God. By this inspiration Peter, beginning with the situation of Judas and the sermon at Pentecost, set the precedent of using the scriptures to validate all that was happening.

This made perfect sense because in this sermon Peter was speaking to Jews. They were likely familiar with the passage in Joel that Peter referenced, but the fact that it was pointing to Jesus was new to them.

Throughout the book of Acts, the apostles' approach was simple: If it cannot be validated by Scripture, refuse it; if it is validated by Scripture, don't fight it but yield to it. This fact may explain the value the early church placed on the scriptures. They were devoted to the apostles' teaching and continually gave their time and energy to learning the scriptures (Acts 6:4).

- How have I viewed the role of the Holy Spirit in broadening my understanding of Holy Scripture?

- In what ways might I raise my expectation for the Spirit to deepen my hunger for the Word of God?

DIG DEEPER · *Acts 1:15–22; 4:24–31*

Father, thank you for the Word of God and for the Spirit you give to guide us into your truth. Open my eyes by your Spirit to see the things that are hidden and let me value your Word as Jesus and his disciples valued it.

PLUNGED INTO PRAYER

DAY 12   *ACTS 2:41–42*

The Holy Spirit will draw you deeper into fellowship with God and with others, and he will do this especially through the exercise of prayer.

There was a reason these believers devoted themselves to prayer. Many of them had seen the way their Lord was devoted to prayer. When they saw this value in Jesus' life, they asked him to teach them to pray. They wanted to pray, not like the Pharisees whom they had seen praying in the marketplace, but like Jesus, who seemed to truly commune with God.

Jesus taught them that prayer is an invitation into the heart and mission of God. Prayer is both the peace and joy of personal communion with God and the struggle of kingdom advancement. There is a beautiful tension in prayer: God is sovereign, yet he asks us to pray, and he works to bring his will to Earth through the prayers of men and women. We work with God to affect our world.

Prayer is instinctual. Our first breath is a cry for help, help that must come from outside ourselves. And yet, real prayer must be learned. Mostly it is learned by doing it with others.

To pray is to change, as Paul says, "*And we all, with unveiled face, beholding the glory of the Lord, are being transformed into the same image from one degree of glory to another. For this comes from the Lord who is the Spirit."* (2 Corinthians 3:18)

But there is a corporate piece to this learning. "And we all" indicates that it is not only personal change, but corporate change. We see our Lord in community and we as a community are changed so that we are like him.

- What difference might I see in my life if my spiritual goal was to pray with greater authority and success one year from now than I do currently?

- What change might happen in me as I experience God in prayer together with others, and not merely in personal prayer?

DIG DEEPER · *Acts 1:12–14; 12:1–17*

Father, my heart longs to pray as Jesus prayed. Teach me to be like him as I behold his face together with others. Let me learn to pray well as I pray with my brothers and sisters.

THE HOUR OF PRAYER

DAY 13   *ACTS 3:1–10*

Peter and John went to the temple at the hour of prayer.

After becoming Christ-followers, they did not stop meeting in the temple. And what did they pray in the temple? Mostly, they prayed the psalms. Prayer in the psalms included exclamations of deep praise, laments, complaints to Yahweh, appeals for justice, requests for daily needs, and calling on the Lord in all seasons of life. The kind of prayer we pray depends on the need of the moment.

The first step in prayer is to listen. Tune in to find the frequency of God. Like radio signals, he is always transmitting, but we are not always listening. Second, we respond with the kind of prayer that is necessary. Prayer in the psalms was sometimes peaceful and pensive, sometimes pushy and persistent.

And prayer in the early church was not merely of the personal kind; it was prayer with others. They were dedicated to communion with God together. It was a lifestyle, with a specific meeting time in a specific place, the temple.

They prayed because they understood their need for communion with God.

They prayed together because they understood their need for communion with one another.

They prayed for things to be as they should be—for their Lord's kingdom to come and his will to be done. They were so immersed in the flurry of activity of the Holy Spirit that when they encountered a specific situation, they knew together what prayer to pray, what action to take.

- What are my rhythms of prayer, personally and with others?

- Do I expect the Holy Spirit to lead me into different kinds of prayer depending on the situation? How good am I at listening for his call?

DIG DEEPER · *EPHESIANS 6:18–20; COLOSSIANS 4:2–6*

Father, I know that prayer is communion with you and also fellowship with others around me. Help us to discern together what is needed in each situation and to work with you to make a way for your kingdom to come more fully here on Earth.

HOW DO I PRAY?

DAY 14   *ROMANS 8:26–27*

These verses give us hope because even the great apostle had times when he was weak, times when he did not know how to pray. When we have no strength and don't know how to pray, the Spirit helps us.

It is encouraging, though hard to imagine, that the apostle who was so educated, so gifted, who literally saw and heard the call of Jesus at his conversion, had the same problem that we do. He faltered and sometimes failed to discern the Father's will.

The Spirit "helps" us. The word used in the original Greek language is *synantilambanomai*, which means, "to take hold of something opposite together". Think of trying to move a large couch. You would need someone on the other side to help you lift. They take hold of it opposite you and lift with you.

This is just what the Spirit does as we are bearing the burdens of our heavy load. He supports, comes alongside, and lends his strength, without which we could never accomplish the task.

But exactly how does the Spirit help us in prayer? First he stirs our hearts with the burden of the Father's heart (the why of prayer). Then he stirs our minds (the what of prayer).

We often don't know what to pray for, but the Spirit brings it to mind, and even intercedes for us with prayers beyond our words. This is a beautiful part of abiding in Christ. As we are connected to the vine, the sap flows through us and out of us, back to God. We work together for his purposes.

- Do I expect the Spirit to lead me in prayer? To pray for me and through me?
- In what ways do I need the Spirit's help to pray today?

DIG DEEPER · *1 Corinthians 2:11–14; John 15:1–16*

Father, I confess that many times I do not know how I should pray. But I thank you that you have given the precious gift of your Spirit to come alongside and take hold of this task with me. Give me the help I need to pray your will today.

MADE HOLY BY THE SPIRIT

DAY 15   *ACTS 5:1–11*

The Spirit will separate the precious from the worthless in our lives. John the Baptist said the Messiah would baptize with the Holy Ghost and fire. His winnowing fork is in his hand and he is skillful in clearing out his threshing floor, John warned. And Paul taught that there are fruits that prove our repentance (Acts 26:19–20).

When the enemy could not stop the church by persecution from without, his next attempt was to attack it from within. Historically, pressure from without only strengthens and spreads the church. So the greatest danger to the church is not persecution but false motives, toleration of sin, and division.

The Holy Spirit works to make his church holy. On this highway of holiness he will bring us the easiest way we will go—but he will surely bring us. Being conformed to the image of the Son is our destiny. There must be a distinction between the followers of Jesus and the unbelievers, and here in the early church we see that revival and holiness go hand in hand.

Great fear came upon not only the church, but all those who heard about the purification of the church. Part of this fear of the Lord, we are told, is a hatred of evil (Proverbs

8:13). This is the mark of a person—and a church—in which the Holy Spirit is active.

- What process is the Spirit taking me through to purge me of what is worthless in my life?
- The unsaved held the church in high esteem (Acts 5:13). When was the last time an unbeliever marveled at my integrity?

DIG DEEPER · *LUKE 3:15–18; TITUS 3:4–8*

Father, holiness is something that is foreign to me in my own power. But it is something I long for and something the Spirit works in me. Bring the power of your Holy Spirit to burn out the chaff in my life.

THROUGH EVERY BELIEVER

DAY 16   *ACTS 6:1–7*

One evidence of the Spirit's work in the early church was the distribution of different gifts in every believer. Though we see the work of the Spirit through the main leaders of the church, it is also clear that everyone is important and the Spirit works through each member of the body of Christ.

The seven men chosen were full of faith and the character of Christ and empowered to meet practical needs that crossed ethnic boundaries. By their wisdom and willingness to serve the larger body of Christ, they prevented division from tearing the early church apart. Many such women are also named in the New Testament.

As the church's influence spread, we see people influencing through their individual gifts. Barnabas was an extraordinary man who had a tremendous influence on the early church. Though his name was Joseph, they nicknamed him Barnabas—*"son of encouragement"*—because he operated in this gift of encouragement.

We owe Barnabas a tremendous debt of gratitude, for his behind-the-scenes ministry of encouragement was pivotal in influencing the early church. You can expect the Spirit to anoint your uniqueness to spread God's kingdom around you.

- Have I had the mindset that only "leaders" can be used in the church?
- What unique gifts and passions has God given me to bless others?

DIG DEEPER · *Acts 4:36; Ephesians 4:11–16*

Father, I thank you that you made me unique in personality, abilities, and spiritual gifts. Empower me today to use my uniqueness in a supernatural way to bless others and extend your kingdom.

KEEPING IN STEP WITH THE SPIRIT

DAY 17　　　　　*Acts 10:1–33*

Two very different men from different nationalities living in different cities: Yet they both reached out to the God of Heaven. And God put their paths together in an extraordinary way.

Cornelius had a heart that was seeking God, but had not yet heard of God's way of salvation, Jesus. As he prayed, he saw a vision and heard an angel's voice speak to him with specific direction. He acted on it immediately.

Peter was still struggling with those words he had heard Jesus say, that the gospel would go to all nations. While he prayed he also saw a vision telling him to change his way of thinking and that God had a mission for him. Like Cornelius, he followed the leading of the Holy Spirit.

It is the Spirit who gives us life and also shows us how to live it. Such a life is one of learning to listen to, submit to, and shadow the very heart and will of God. We are called into a vibrant relationship, a co-working with God toward his purposes.

Though our natures gravitate toward the opposite (keeping in step with our own desires), this kind of Spirit-living is possible through God's empowering. Jesus lived by doing only what he saw the Father do and speaking what he heard the Father speak.

Since we have the precious presence of the Spirit inside us, we are privileged to pay attention and to align with him—to let him lead as we dance with him.

- The Holy Spirit is a leader. Am I living in expectation that he will lead me throughout my day?

- Have I been more comfortable following a list of rules than following the Spirit's leading? How can I move from a life of mere legalistic dos and don'ts to a life of listening and submitting to the Spirit?

DIG DEEPER · *GALATIANS 5:16–25; LUKE 4:1*

Father, what a privilege it is to be filled with your very presence and made alive to you by your Spirit. Make me sensitive to the leadership of your Spirit; compel me and constrain me as you wish, for your glory.

THE SPIRIT HELPS OUR MARRIAGES

DAY 18   *EPHESIANS 5:18–33*

Weddings are wonderful occasions—the birth of a new family, the beauty of the bride, the celebration of a pledge of lifelong commitment. It is the culmination of months (maybe years) of planning, hoping, and dreaming, and it all crescendos on this one day.

But after the wedding comes the marriage. And that is an entirely different thing. Marriage and parenting (instructions on which follow today's passage) are perhaps the most daily things most of us deal with, and daily things are the hardest. They require making decisions each day—many times a day—that are consistent with our vows.

Keeping the vows we spoke on the wedding day requires a commitment and a power that is beyond us. The commands for husbands and wives are nestled into the context of the work of the Spirit in our marriages. And no wonder we need the Spirit, for who, in their own power, could treat their spouses as we are instructed to in this passage? How can there be mutual submission and love, the kind that lays itself down for another, without the full working of the Spirit inside us?

The wisdom preacher in Ecclesiastes challenges us to do everything our hand finds to do with all of our might. And he says this in the context of marriage: *"Enjoy life with the wife whom you love, all the days of your vain life that he has given you under the sun."* (Ecclesiastes 9:9–10)

It is as if the preacher is saying, "If you are going to be married, don't settle for mediocrity—go for excellence." This excellence is dependent on the work of the Spirit.

- In what ways do I see my need for the Spirit's help in my marriage and parenting?

- Do I expect the Spirit to empower me to love and respect my spouse? How can I receive that help day-to-day?

DIG DEEPER · *Ecclesiastes 9:9–10; Colossians 3:12–19*

Father, I pray for my marriage and the marriages of those around me. Only through your power can I play the Jesus role and honor my spouse above myself. Give me what I need to experience supernatural love and an extraordinary marriage.

MEETING THE NEEDS OF THE BODY

DAY 19   *ROMANS 12:3–8*

What a genius God is! He immerses followers of Jesus into one body and empowers each member to meet the needs of other members. He does this by distributing supernatural gifts by the work of the Spirit.

Consider how well we are cared for by these gifted people:

- The *prophet* keeps us centered on the things that are important to God's mission, meeting the spiritual needs of the body.

- The *servant* keeps the day-by-day work of ministry moving, meeting the practical needs of the body.

- The *teacher* keeps us focused on truth, meeting the mental needs of the body.

- The *exhorter* sees potential and encourages us, meeting the psychological needs of the body.

- The *giver* generously shares resources, meeting the material needs of the body.

- The *administrator* provides leadership and organization, meeting the functional needs of the body.

- The *mercy person* provides empathy and personal support, meeting the emotional needs of the body.

Each gift is a manifestation of the heart of Christ. Christ the Prophet is present to his body through the prophetic gift. Christ the Teacher guides us into truth through the teaching gift. Christ the Giver provides for the needs of his body through the gift of giving.

The Holy Spirit distributes the heart and actions of Jesus through these supernatural gifts, given for the members of his body and for those not yet saved. What a genius God is!

- In what ways have I seen the heart and works of Jesus through the gifts of those around me?

- What gifts has the Spirit given to me to bless others with?

DIG DEEPER · *1 Corinthians 12:1–13;
Ephesians 4:7–14*

*Father, your wisdom is amazing. I see the beauty
of Jesus through the gifts of his followers. Thank
you for generously giving gifts to your body
through the Spirit. Empower me to use my gifts
to be a blessing to others today.*

NEW BIRTH

DAY 20   *ACTS 2:37–39*

It is impossible to come into a relationship with God except through the work of the Holy Spirit. Conviction of sin, awareness of our need for a Savior, revelation of Jesus, and the regeneration of our souls only happen by supernatural means.

Any truth we come to know about Jesus Christ, ourselves, and salvation, we come to know only through the active revelation of the Spirit. The listeners of the Pentecost sermon, through the preaching of God's word and the inherent power of the gospel message, experienced the cutting open of their hearts. The Spirit is dynamic and precise in his heart surgery.

The prophet Ezekiel spoke this heart work when he declared the New Covenant that God would make with his people. This would be a covenant not based on our performance, but on God's work, for God's glory alone.

"And I will give you a new heart, and a new spirit I will put within you. And I will remove the heart of stone from your flesh and give you a heart of flesh. And I will put my Spirit within you, and cause you to walk in my statutes and be careful to obey my rules." (Ezekiel 36:26–27)

Jesus said it is not possible to see the Kingdom of God unless we are born of the Spirit (John 3:3–5). We do nothing in our own power to be born physically; it is the work of another. The same is true of spiritual birth. It is the work of the Spirit so that God will receive all the glory.

- Have I experienced the convicting and renewing work of the Holy Spirit?
- In my mind, is my standing before God dependent on my own performance, or on the finished work of Jesus and the regenerative work of the Spirit?

DIG DEEPER · *JOHN 3:3–8; TITUS 3:4–7*

Father, I am grateful for the peace that comes from the knowledge that my salvation is the work of your Spirit and not of my own merit. As the Spirit has convicted and drawn me to Jesus, may he continue to draw me close and make me alive to your will.

BEARS FRUIT IN US

DAY 21 | *GALATIANS 5:22–25*

The Holy Spirit causes the life of Christ inside us to come forth in simple, beautiful, God-like ways. The indwelling Christ seeps out from our inner motivations through our outward actions toward others. But the source is not our own strength or power.

This practical life of the Spirit develops from a life source. The source is Christ within us, and the fruit that comes is the work of the Holy Spirit. Christ-likeness becomes reality by the sovereign work of the Spirit.

In the early church we see this Spirit-fruit embodied in the actions of believers:

- Love is poured out in our hearts by the Spirit. (Romans 5:5)

- Joy filled the disciples' hearts by the Spirit. (Acts 13:52)

- Peace and unity come through the Spirit. (Ephesians 4:3)

And in the same way, each of these character traits listed in Galatians is linked to the active work of the Holy Spirit inside of us. The beautiful truth is that I don't strive to make these things a reality in my life. My job is to rest in the finished work of Jesus.

Rather than trying to change from the outside in, we rely on the truth of the gospel: That our old, stony heart was removed and a new heart was put into us. Through this exchange we now have the kind of heart that causes us to follow after and act like God.

- Have I been characterized by striving to produce this kind of character in my life?
- Do I find myself resting in the finished work of Jesus on the cross and the ongoing work of the Spirit to bear the fruit of righteousness in me?

DIG DEEPER · *John 15:1–17; Psalm 1:1–3*

Father, thank you for the great work of the Spirit
that brings this God-like character into my life.
Help me to not strive or focus on my performance,
but rather to rest in the life of Christ inside me
and the Spirit's work.

THE SPIRIT SPEAKS TO US

DAY 22   *ACTS 8:26–40*

Regular people such as you and I can hear the voice of God. It is usually not his audible voice, but an inaudible voice that sometimes seems louder than the audible voice, for it shakes us deeply and changes things inside us.

There are many biblical ways God speaks to us, most importantly through the inspired scriptures. But in these scriptures we see that God also speaks through prayer and nature, through spiritual gifts, through dreams and visions, through circumstances, and through the community of believers.

But here in this passage we see the Spirit also speaks directly to us at times. In fact, Philip was spoken to by the angel of the Lord *and* by the Spirit. We could say that obedience to the voice of the angel put him in a position to hear the voice of the Spirit. So we learn to hear God's voice better as we obey what we have already heard.

And as Philip responded to the voice of the Spirit, he opened his mouth to declare the written Word of God. It seems that the manifold ways that God speaks are often interrelated.

The beautiful truth is, the Holy Spirit speaks not only to the church body and not only in general directive terms, but personally, specifically, and immediately in our present moment. Jesus taught us, "My sheep hear my voice, and I know them, and they follow me." (John 10:27)

- Do I create space in my daily life to hear the voice of God?
- How can I better position myself to hear the voice of God through the Word, community, and prayer?

DIG DEEPER · *Hebrews 11:1–2; 1 Kings 19:11–13*

What a wonder that the God of the Universe has chosen to speak to his children through the Holy Spirit. Father, give me ears to hear and a heart of expectancy for what you might say to me. Give me grace to obey what I hear.

OUR GUIDE INTO TRUTH

DAY 23 | *JOHN 16:12–15*

There is an assault on truth today. Things that are logical and obvious are being rejected, and things that are completely against science and reason are being held as truth. How do we walk in confidence that we know the truth? How did the early church walk in their own day of deception?

The present and active Holy Spirit takes the things that pertain to Jesus and his kingdom and discloses them to us. In this way, he keeps the truth before us and leads us in it.

Jesus, the Great Shepherd, was aware of the capacity of his sheep. He knew that there were things they needed to know but did not have the ability to grasp at the time. In his patience, he waited; in his generosity, he gave the Spirit as a guide.

"And I will ask the Father, and he will give you another Helper, to be with you forever, even the Spirit of truth, whom the world cannot receive, because it neither sees him nor knows him. You know him, for he dwells with you and will be in you." (John 14:16–17)

Today, technology and the deceit of man make it increasingly difficult to know what is true and what is false. But as believers in Jesus, we have a superpower: the Spirit of truth who dwells inside us. There is a way to hear the voice

OUR GUIDE IN GRIEF

DAY 25   *2 CORINTHIANS 1:3–5*

mised that the Spirit he would send would be a
r (John 14:16, KJV).

church had many victories to celebrate. But they
nced the struggles of living in a culture that was
heir faith and lifestyle. Paul encouraged these
rs that God would comfort them and then give
of turning to comfort others.

to all of us in a broken world. The psalmists
r pain and fear, anger and loss in the most
The early believers were very familiar with
hey knew that prayers are not always polite,
times, the psalms of lament give us freedom
vhat we are feeling. They even give us the
en we can't find our own.

e us the words; the Spirit gives us the
y to see things from God's perspective.
rts us in our grief, but guides us toward
ut our difficult times. He gently leads us
have in Jesus. He sets us in a solid place
elp others.

s and anger and fears to God is not a
uest kind of faith, for in our pain, we
away from him.

---

of our Shepherd; there is a way to know truth and walk in it. He has not left us as orphans; he has come to us. He walks with us and guides us in truth by his Spirit.

- Do I feel a measure of fear because of the confusing voices of my culture? Do I believe the Spirit of Truth will guide me?

- What disciplines am I employing to quiet myself to hear the voice of truth?

DIG DEEPER · *1 JOHN 4:1–6; JOHN 14:16–18*

Father, I need to hear your voice of truth in the midst of the confusing and deceiving voices of my day. I thank you for not leaving me as an orphan, and I trust your goodness to guide me today.

OUR GUIDE TO BEING RIGHT WITH GOD

DAY 24   *John 16:7–11*

It is a good thing to be convicted of our sin. It is the grace of God that he gives us the gift of a conscience, that inner feeling or voice that acts as a guide to the rightness or wrongness of our behavior and motives.

It seems that the Holy Spirit's job is both to comfort the afflicted and afflict the comfortable. Jesus told his disciples it would be profitable for him to leave them and send the Spirit. The Spirit is specifically profitable to us in his role to convict us, or open our eyes, in three areas:

- Sin: He shows us what is wrong so we can be made right by turning to Christ.

- Righteousness: He shows us what is right so we can follow it.

- Judgment: He shows us that there is a day of reckoning scheduled, a day in which the holy God will mete out justice and rid his creation of all sin. All who reject Christ and remain in their sin will be condemned along with Satan, and this is the warning that the Holy Spirit sounds in the hearts of the unsaved.

- How have I felt the comfort of the Holy Spirit in my dark times? What part of my own pain can I bring to him now?

- How might the Spirit use me to comfort others who are suffering today?

DIG DEEPER · *1 Thessalonians 5:14; John 14:15–18*

Father, I thank you for the Spirit who comforts and helps in my times of deepest need. Help me to turn to you to receive the comfort I need and open my eyes to those around me who also need comfort.

WHICH WAY DO WE GO?

DAY 26 · *ACTS 15:1–35*

What do we do when we face a situation we have never faced before? When the wisdom we need in order to respond is not within us? This is the situation the early church leaders faced.

This tension between following Christ and keeping the law was crucial to get right. The church leaders called the first council at Jerusalem to deal with the situation. There was no shortage of opinions on the matter, but they needed to get the mind of the Lord.

As the early church leaders came together to listen, the Spirit spoke in a threefold way to give them the guidance they needed:

- The obvious work of the Spirit: The leaders listened to the reports of Peter, Paul, and Barnabas as they told of the works of the Holy Spirit among the Gentiles.

- The Word of God: James stood up with an interpretation of the prophet Amos concerning the blessing of David being for the Gentiles. (vs 16–18)

- The agreement of the brothers: "For it has seemed good to the Holy Spirit and to us..." (vs 28)

The old adage "follow your heart" is not always good advice. It depends on the state of your heart. Proverbs tells us that, "*There is a way that seems right to a man, but its end is the way to death.*" (Proverbs 14:12) It is better to lead your heart with the Word of God and learn to hear the voice of the Spirit together with others.

- What matter am I facing today that needs direction from the Holy Spirit?

- How might the Spirit be using the Word of God and my Christian community to help guide me?

DIG DEEPER · *Acts 4:18–31; 1:15–26*

*Father, I know I don't have the wisdom inside me
for all the decisions I am facing today. But I am
confident that the Wise One lives inside me. I quiet
myself to listen to your Word and to my brothers and
sisters that I may hear your guidance.*

HOLY SPIRIT STOPS US

DAY 27 · *ACTS 16:6–7*

Jesus told his twelve to go into all the world and make disciples. Paul, too, heard a similar call. But while Paul was going in obedience, the Spirit said, "Stop." This must have seemed strange to Paul, for he was going to preach the gospel where it had not yet been heard. And yet the Spirit clearly said, "No."

Paul was forbidden to go some places and pushed toward others. No wonder he would later write to the Galatians that the Christian life is not one of conforming to outward standards, but of walking with the Spirit (see Galatians 5).

In fact, the Spirit ended or redirected lots of activity in the early church. He stopped Philip from participating in a revival so he could send him to an Ethiopian eunuch who was hungry for God (Acts 8).

He stopped the disciples from attending the needs of widows and had them appoint faith-filled men to that task so they could continue focusing on the Word of God and prayer (Acts 6).

Later the Spirit stopped Paul's entire traveling ministry and landed him in jail because he had some important letters for him to write. We are still reading those letters today. When the Spirit says stop, we must stop, for he has higher purposes.

- Have I ever felt the urge of the Holy Spirit to stop a certain activity or project? Did I obey?
- In what ways can I better hear these kinds of promptings?

DIG DEEPER · *Acts 8:4–40; 6:1–7*

*Father, what a wonderful gift you have given us
in a Helper that will guide us in where to go and
where to not go, and when to stop and redirect. May
my heart always be tuned to your frequency, and
may I have grace to obey the haltings of the Spirit.*

HOLY SPIRIT PUSHES US

DAY 28 | *ACTS 16:8–10*

Paul and Barnabas were stopped by the Spirit from preaching in Asia not once but twice. Perhaps when we are rebuked repeatedly we are more prone to be apprehensive and halting in our next move. This is natural.

But the Holy Spirit is a help and a guide, and he is faithful to redirect our steps in the way of his own will. For Paul, it was through a dream: a man, a city, and a desperate call for help. Paul immediately responded, and the door for the gospel to spread into Europe was opened.

The Spirit both constrains and compels, pulls us back and pushes us forward. Our job is to pay attention and obey. This wasn't the first time he had urged the church leaders forward. Though Jesus said the gospel message was to be preached beyond Jerusalem, the Spirit had to push them out of their place of comfort by the persecution that arose after Stephen's death.

Another time, while the leaders of the church at Antioch were worshiping the Lord and fasting, the Spirit spoke to them to send out two of their best into the mission he had ordained for them (Acts 13). This was the beginning for the ministry team of Paul and Barnabas. When the Spirit says go, we must go. Only then will we experience the grace and power for our mission.

- Have I ever felt the urge of the Holy Spirit to go in a certain direction or do a certain thing? Did I obey?

- What might hinder me from stepping out in obedience to the call to go?

DIG DEEPER · *ACTS 13:1–3; 8:1–4*

Father, I long to hear you clearly and to have courage to step into whatever you are calling me to. Speak to me, give me vision, and empower me to go forward at your call.

SPIRIT OF ADOPTION

DAY 29 | *ROMANS 8:16–17*

Because we live in a broken world, the word "father" may not be a positive word for many. *Father* may be connected to words like desertion, divorce, abuse, demands, or silence.

But the Bible teaches that we have been adopted into an eternal family where the Father is different. This heavenly Father is loving, good, stable, truthful, generous, just, reliable, merciful, and kind. It is the Holy Spirit who convinces us of this truth and makes it a reality in our daily lives.

Adoption is really at the heart of the gospel: "*and I will be a father to you, and you shall be sons and daughters to me, says the Lord Almighty.*" (2 Corinthians 6:18) What gets passed on by parent to child is more than just resources. Our place in the family also has to do with identity and acceptance, affirmation and love. The Spirit of the Lord rests on us. Like Jesus, we hear his voice, and he calls us beloved children (Matthew 3:16–17).

In Christ we have a unique and intimate relationship with our Father God. We become part of the family, so every other believer becomes our brother and sister. We have an inheritance that is eternal. And this new status changes the way we view God and people. It affects everything we do. Through the Holy Spirit we bear witness to our sonship and we cry out, as children, to our "papa".

- Have I heard the voice of the Father call out to me as he did to Jesus, "You are my beloved son/daughter, I love you, I am pleased with you"?

- How might the way I view God, pray to him, worship him, and minister for him change as the Spirit opens my eyes to my spiritual adoption?

DIG DEEPER · *GALATIANS 4:4–7; MATTHEW 3:16–17*

*Father, thank you for your great love that calls to me,
changes me, and welcomes me into your eternal family.
Teach me to release the old orphan ways and to think
and live like a beloved child.*

THE SPIRIT RESURRECTS US

DAY 30   *ROMANS 8:9–11*

The same Spirit that raised Jesus from the dead dwells in every believer. And it is through this Spirit that our eternal life is made real and tangible, for *"he who raised Christ Jesus from the dead will also give life to your mortal bodies through his Spirit who dwells in you."* (Romans 8:11b)

This is one precious part of the unsearchable riches we have in Christ. For when we were dead in our sin, God raised us up together with Jesus. We don't have to fear death, for the Spirit of Life will make us alive forever.

Jesus tried to explain this to Nicodemus during a conversation they had one dark, quiet night. In order to see the Kingdom of Heaven, we must be born of the Spirit. The Holy Spirit does his work of regenerating my spirit so I am alive to God. But that is not where he stops. He will also make my mortal body come alive in the resurrection.

The same Spirit that makes us alive spiritually will raise our bodies and change them so we will live forever in glorified bodies. *"So is it with the resurrection of the dead. What is sown is perishable; what is raised is imperishable."* (1 Corinthians 15:42) What a beautiful promise we have, that we will live forever by the Spirit of God.

- Does this promise of life through the Spirit change the way I view death?

- Is the hope of resurrection alive within me? Who is around me today who needs this hope?

DIG DEEPER · *EPHESIANS 1:15–2:7; 1 CORINTHIANS 15:40–46*

Father, I thank you for the life-giving, regenerative work of the Holy Spirit. Thank you that you have made me alive when I was spiritually dead. And thank you that you will raise my mortal body up to immortality by the same Spirit. Thank you that death has been defeated!

AFTERWORD

Jesus is still speaking and acting today. The time we take to interact with him demonstrates our faith in that statement. If we truly believe that God speaks and that what he has to say is worth hearing, what space are we creating in our lives for interaction with him?

The spiritual disciplines are where our theology intersects with our everyday lives.

- We believe God *speaks*, so we take time to listen.

- We believe God is *omnipresent*, so we acknowledge and sense his presence.

- We believe God is *active*, so we look and listen for his activity.

- We believe God is *all wise*, so we seek his wisdom.

- We believe God is *our shepherd*, so we allow him to lead us.

- We believe God is *a rewarder of those who diligently seek him*, so we seek him.

If you have finished the readings in this book, you have disciplined yourself to encounter God's grace through his Word, through prayer, and through meditation. I want to commend you for your diligence and challenge you to continue.

The source of these readings are my personal journals, written over a period of many decades. My encouragement to you is that you can also find your own treasures from the Word of God, from prayer, and from journaling what you are seeing in the scriptures and the things God is working into your life by his Spirit.

What if you began (or continued) a practice of seeing the beauty of the Father, the faithfulness of the Son, and the activity of the Spirit day by day? What if you journaled what you see? What if, some time in the future, you put your musings into written form and passed them along to your family, your friends, or even a broader audience God might open to you?

As surely as I can do this, you can do it. You can spread the knowledge of God, the fragrance of Jesus, the fellowship of the Spirit to those around you. In the end, we are called to know the Triune God and to make him known. You have insights and experiences I don't have. There are others who need to hear the hope-filled insight that God is working into your life.

Drink him in…pass him on. There is so much of him to know!

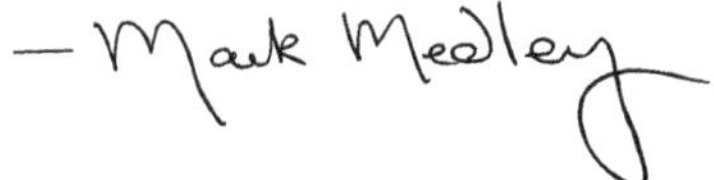

ABOUT THE AUTHOR

Mark Medley is a father, pastor, author, musician, and international Bible teacher who loves life in his beautiful native East Tennessee. Mark has been on the pastoral staff at Trinity Community Church in Knoxville since 1989. He is the founder of Thrive Ministries, a cooperative of international pastors, church overseers, and five-fold ministers who work together in multiplying healthy leaders worldwide. Learn more at **www.markmedley.org**.